AIRCRAFT DOWN

AIRCRAFT DOWN
Forced Landings, Crash Landings and Rescues

Alec Brew

Pen & Sword
AVIATION

First published in Great Britain in 2005 by
Pen & Sword Aviation
an imprint of
Pen & Sword Books Ltd
47 Church Street
Barnsley
South Yorkshire
S70 2AS

Copyright © Alec Brew 2005

ISBN 1 84415 240 5

A CIP catalogue record for this book is
available from the British Library

Typeset in Plantin by
Pen & Sword Books Ltd incorporates the imprints of Pen & Sword
Aviation, Pen & Sword Maritime, Pen & Sword Military, Wharncliffe
Local History, Pen & Sword Select, Pen & Sword Military Classics and
Leo Cooper.

For a complete list of Pen & Sword titles please contact
Pen & Sword Books Limited
47 Church Street, Barnsley, South Yorkshire, S70 2AS, England
E-mail: enquiries@pen-and-sword.co.uk
Website: www.pen-and-sword.co.uk

CONTENTS

Introduction 7

Chapter 1   Down in the Irish Sea 9
Chapter 2   Down on the Railway 18
Chapter 3   Down in the Sahara 22
Chapter 4   Down on Lake Tanganyika 27
Chapter 5   Down on the Ice Pack 34
Chapter 6   Down in the Atlantic 47
Chapter 7   Down in Outback 58
Chapter 8   Down in an Ornamental Lake 69
Chapter 9   Down in the Desert and Down in the Sea 73
Chapter 10   Down in the Channel 84
Chapter 11   Down in the North Sea 92
Chapter 12   Down on the Dark Peak 102
Chapter 13   Pancake in the Black Country 108
Chapter 14   Down in Greenland 113
Chapter 15   Downed Lady 117
Chapter 16   Down in the Arctic Ocean 122
Chapter 17   A Dip in the Med 127
Chapter 18   Down on the Tundra 132
Chapter 19   Down in the Peak District 140
Chapter 20   What You Do When the Engine Falls Off 147
Chapter 21   To Bale Out or Not to Bale Out 155
Chapter 22   Down in the Yukon 163
Chapter 23   Down in the Oman 168

Index 173

Acknowledgements

Many of the photographs in this book came from the West Midland Aviation Archive, at the Boulton Paul Aircraft Heritage Project. Others to whom I owe thanks are Wing Commander Eric Barwell, Jim Boulton, A/E 'Ben' Gunn, Alex Henshaw, Fred Owen, Group Captain Edwin Shipley, Jenny Woodall, and last but certainly not least Wendy Matthiason.

Introduction

'What goes up must come down' has been a basic concern of aviators since aviation began; specifically returning to earth in the same condition as they went aloft, and hopefully in a place of their own choosing. Although it is often said that a good landing is one you can walk away from, most aviators aim for something better than that.

Terminology comes into play in the difference between a forced landing and a crash-landing. The former suggests an unplanned descent without damage necessarily resulting. The latter suggests damage but not necessarily away from the place you first intended. A crash simply suggests both damage and a lack of intent on the part of the pilot.

The episodes chosen in this book on the whole describe forced landings in out-of-the-way places, usually with damage resulting. In every case the pilot and crew survived the forced landing, and awaited their rescue. In most of the events described, rescue eventually came, sometimes after a very long period of time. Occasionally, rescue was not a problem, despite the unusual location of the forced landing; mostly it involved a long wait, or strenuous efforts by the crew themselves. In a couple of the episodes chosen, rescue never came.

When any pilot experiences a sudden loud bang, or total silence, they are often faced with the stark choice of taking to their parachute, or trying to get their aircraft down in as few pieces as possible. Usually, only military pilots or test pilots have the luxury of the parachute option. Some of the chapters in the book describe the careers of pilots who, faced with this option, have at different times made different choices. Civilian pilots usually have to resort to prayer and holding back a rising flood of panic, as they scan the ground for likely options, and work out how much they are still in control.

Flying is often described as 99 per cent boredom, and 1 per cent blind panic. These are the stories of some of those 1 per cents.

CHAPTER 1

Down in the Irish Sea

Even those with a limited knowledge of aviation history know that Louis Blériot was the first to fly the English Channel, or that Commander Read in his NC-4 flying boat was the first to fly the Atlantic, but who first flew the Irish Sea is less well known. This is probably because the question has three answers, all of them correct – well it is the Irish Sea. The man most commonly acknowledged to have first flown the Irish Sea is Robert Loraine. In fact, he never made it. He force-landed in the sea and had to swim the last part of the way to Ireland! Not only that, before he had even reached the taking off point, he force-landed in one of the remotest areas of Wales.

Robert Loraine was famous even before his flying exploits, being one of the best known actors of his day. He had been a soldier in the Boer War, and was interested in flying from its earliest days. He had watched Henri Farman flying at Issy-les-Moulineaux, and when Louis Blériot climbed into his monoplane to fly the Channel for the first time, it was Loraine to whom he handed the crutches he was using at the time. Blériot's achievement inspired Loraine to to to the Blériot School to learn to fly. However, his impetuous nature caused too many crashes, and it was at the Farman School at Mourmelons where he earned his Aviator's Certificate on 21 June 1910.

Unwilling to wait for delivery of a new Farman biplane, he offered Farman the huge sum of £7000 for one that had already been sold but was awaiting collection. He was able to pay so much because he had recently earned £40,000 for a production of George Bernard Shaw's *Man and Superman*. He engaged Jules Vedrines as his mechanic, a small acerbic Frenchman who was later to become a famous aviator in his own right.

He transported his new Farman to an airfield that had just been built at Beaulieu in the New Forest. His practice flights from there usually ended in crash-landings, but Vedrines patiently repaired the aircraft each time. The Bournemouth Flying Meeting was due to start on 11 July, following hard on the first of the year held at Dunstall Park, Wolverhampton. Loraine wished to make a good impression by flying to the Meeting, whereas all the other competitors were transporting their aircraft down from the Midlands by rail. Unfortunately, Loraine crashed his Farman on the way to Bournemouth and it arrived as a pile of wreckage in six farm carts!

Vedrines worked his magic once more, and the Farman was ready in time for Loraine to make the most meritorious flight of the Meeting, when he flew to the Isle of Wight in the midst of a thunderstorm. He was flying under the pseudonym Robert Jones, as he did not wish his flying to be seen as a publicity stunt. The Press were soon to discover the truth, but he persisted with the ruse, though it brought him more publicity than if he had used his own name. He even insisted in signing autographs as Jones, whenever he adopted the role of aviator.

The Bournemouth Flying Meeting finished under a cloud when the Wright biplane of Charles Rolls broke up in the air and he was killed. The next Meeting was to be held at Blackpool, and Loraine, Vedrines, and his newly appointed manager, George Smart, headed North. After a long delay when the railway 'lost' the Farman, finally found by Smart in a siding 7 miles from Blackpool, Loraine once more made the most impressive flight of the Meeting. On 1 August he flew south over Liverpool and New Brighton, but was forced down with engine trouble at St Anne's on Sea on the way back, continuing after repairs. He was much aggrieved to discover that he had not won the prize for the longest duration in the air, because the whole of the time when he was out of sight of the airfield did not count!

It was in the immediate aftermath of this flight that Loraine hatched his plan to be the first to fly the Irish Sea. On 10 August he took off and headed for Anglesey in beautiful weather. The Farman had been rigged incorrectly and he was forced to push the elevator lever fully forward to keep it flying level. After an hour and a half in the air he saw the Great Orme's Head and a golf course below. He landed successfully, avoiding all the bunkers, a skill he had not attained when holding a golf club rather than a control column. He then waited for Vedrines to arrive and re-rig the aircraft. While he waited he signed autographs as 'Robert Jones' in the clubhouse.

After considerable difficulty clearing a path for take-off through the

1. Robert Loraine taking off from Llandudno golf course on his way to Anglesey.

crowd that had gathered to see the aircraft, Loraine set off again for Anglesey. Hoping to save 15 miles, he decided to cut the corner, rather than hugging the coastline. However, he only had a wrist compass for navigation. This proved entirely useless, and haze soon obscured all sight of land. He flew on for a considerable time, misled by the north-westerly direction of the summer sunset, and then realised he was lost.

He climbed in circles higher and higher, hoping to catch sight of land in one direction or another. When he did it was in an entirely unexpected quarter, and could only be the Isle of Man! He turned back to the south-west, anxious about his fuel supply. His Gnome engine finally stopped when he was about a mile from Anglesey. The coast before him near Carmel Head was rugged, and remote, and as he glided down he searched desperately for a large enough patch of grass on which to land.

He was very lucky to have sufficient height and picked a small, sloping field in a peaceful valley, and managed to make a successful landing, without breaking anything. He was in a field on Bryn Goelcerth Farm, next to the tiny village of Llanfair-yng-Nghorwy, just about the remotest place on the island of Anglesey. He was 16 miles from Holyhead where Vedrines and Smart were waiting anxiously on Salt Island. His flight had been the world's longest oversea flight to that date. His appearance caused something of a sensation in the tiny community, which had been waiting for chapel, on a quiet Sunday evening, only to have arrive in their midst the first flying machine any of them had ever seen.

Llanfair-yng-Nghorwy was so remote it had no proper roads. It was linked to the outside world by cart-tracks, over which transporting the Farman would have been a difficult proposition. As nothing had been broken on landing, Loraine saw no reason not to fly to Ireland the following day. After travelling to Holyhead to inform his assistants, and staying the night, he set off back to the aircraft. Smart travelled with him and he too was not impressed by the remoteness of the location, the last part of the journey being over 8 miles of awful cart-tracks, winding up and down over rocky hillsides, and he concurred with Loraine's decision.

Smart had chartered six tugs to take station along the route, and they sailed one by one from the harbour. The gathered journalists waited on Salt Island for Loraine to fly in and refuel.

Unfortunately, the wind in the little valley was too strong for Loraine to take-off. After two days his impatience got the better of him, and he tried to make the short fifteen-minute flight to Salt Island in spite of the wind. He crashed badly.

He had got the villagers to help him wheel the aircraft to the top of the sloping field, so that the downhill run would help the take-off. However, this also meant that he was taking off downwind. After an over-long run, he had only reached a height of 15 feet. This was insufficient to clear a small rise beyond the field, and he crashed into it. The Farman seemed a total write-off, though he was once more unharmed himself.

The first forced landing on Anglesey had been followed very quickly by the first aircraft crash on Anglesey, and though there was no problem rescuing the pilot, rescuing the aircraft seemed more difficult. There was nothing for it but to build a hangar on the spot, and reconstruct the shattered aircraft. By the superhuman efforts of Vedrines and his brother, who was a skilled carpenter, the Farman was ready on 4 September. After all its crashes, all that remained of the original aircraft was the Gnome engine; everything else had been replaced.

The plan now was to fly directly to Ireland without stopping to refuel at Salt Island. During the rebuilding a new four-hour fuel tank had been fitted, which was more than enough for the journey. As Loraine revved the engine, Vedrines and everyone else who was available held the aircraft back. At Loraine's signal they let go and the wheels rolled a short way, but then cut through the hard surface crust of the field and sank through to the bog that was beneath. The suction of this pulled the undercarriage clean off, and the aircraft crashed to the floor with Loraine's legs trapped beneath the centre-section. Luckily, the engine stopped and there was no fire, as everyone ran to lift the aircraft off Loraine's legs.

Anglesey had now witnessed its second aircraft crash. Loraine's legs were badly bruised but not broken and when Smart informed him that Lord Sheffield had offered him the use of a field at Penhros Park, right next to the water's edge, his enthusiasm was rekindled once more. The wrecked Farman was transported by a humble farm cart to this field, and the faithful Vedrines rebuilt it once again. The following Sunday, 11 September 1910, Robert Loraine was once more ready to go.

He donned two sweaters, a padded waistcoat and a patent jacket made of reindeer hair, which was especially buoyant. As there would be no tugs for

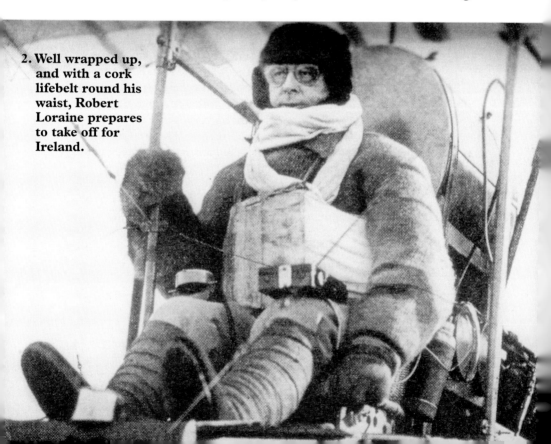

2. Well wrapped up, and with a cork lifebelt round his waist, Robert Loraine prepares to take off for Ireland.

this attempt, his finances being at a low ebb after all his tribulations, he also took the precaution of donning a cork lifebelt, and wore a large whistle round his neck. There was little shipping in the Irish Sea that day, so the whistle was of dubious value. Having learned from the failure of his wrist compass on the flight to Angelsey, he strapped a large box compass to his right knee and a map case to his left.

Loraine climbed aboard the Farman and Smart walked forward to where the level ground fell away. Admiral Burr, the Admiral of the port, shook Loraine's knee in encouragement, that being the only part he could reach. Vedrines started the engine, and Loraine was soon roaring into the air, watched by a line of Penhros Park servants, all holding prayer books! It was Sunday, and they were all on their way to Matins.

With a strong easterly wind his ground speed was high and he hoped to make the crossing in less than an hour and a half. He climbed steadily to about 4000 feet. All of a sudden the engine stopped, and the Farman began plunging towards the sea. Loraine began juggling with the petrol cock, opening it a little and then shutting it in case the Gnome was flooded. Just as he thought he was going to plunge into the cold, harsh Irish Sea the engine spluttered and then fired, and he was able to level out only 20 feet above the waves. He held the aircraft level for a while and then began to regain his altitude.

Once more silence fell, as the engine stopped and the wind whistled through the rigging wires as the aircraft glided towards the unwelcome sea. This time the Gnome picked up again at a higher altitude, and Loraine began climbing once more. Three more times the same thing happened, and as he had not seen a ship or land for fifty minutes, he only hoped and prayed that his compass worked and he was keeping the sun in the right quarter.

About halfway across the sea he ran into a squall of rain, and had difficulty holding the Farman steady. When an hour had passed he began to get nervous. At the altitude he was flying he should have been able to see land, if he was on the right course. But there was nothing. Suddenly, he noticed the Kish light vessel right below him. he knew that this was only 6 miles from Dublin Bay, which must be obscured by haze. Just beyond the light vessel was the Butter boat steaming for Holyhead, and he cheered out loud in relief. He could see the steam from its siren so he knew the crew had seen him, but his feeling of triumph only lasted for three minutes.

He looked at his watch and worked out that he had done 64 miles in only 1 hour and 10 minutes. Suddenly, the Farman began to rise and dip for no apparent reason. He fought to keep control as it banked to the left and right. For at least two minutes he flew along with the aircraft steeply banked to the right. He was soon sweating with the effort of trying to keep it level, but was losing altitude all the time. When he caught sight of Horth Head, to the right, he was down to 500 feet. He turned towards the headland, but by the time he was 100 yards from it he was down to 100 feet, lower than the cliff-tops. He had to turn away, but as he did so, something broke.

The Farman fell straight into the sea. Loraine plunged below the surface, and it seemed ages before he bobbed up. However, because his cork lifebelt had slipped, he was upside down! He struggled to right himself, and found he was alongside the Farman, which was floating upside down with its wheels in the air.

He began swimming towards the lighthouse, struggling to make headway with so many clothes on, but every time he stopped he turned turtle. When he was 50 yards from the shore he saw the lighthouse keeper preparing to come into the sea to rescue him. He desperately yelled that he did not need any help. He wanted to cross the Irish Sea entirely unaided, even the last 50 yards. Every time he stopped swimming to swear and gesticulate to the lighthouse keeper he turned turtle, which only made the keeper more anxious to save him! He finally made the man understand that he did not need any help, and flopped exhaustedly onto the rocky shore.

Robert Loraine had crossed the Irish Sea, but he had missed by a fifth of a mile, doing it all by air. Despite this, it was generally accepted that the crossing had been achieved, and it was not for two years that someone willing to split hairs prepared to repeat the flight.

Loraine's Farman was salvaged and returned to Hendon, but this time it was beyond repair, and he bought two new biplanes. Later in the year he achieved another first when he sent the first wireless message from the air, in a Bristol Boxkite over Salisbury Plain. After his two new aircraft were both wrecked, by a hangar collapse and an explosion, he gave up aviation for a while and returned to the stage to renew his shattered finances.

It was not until April 1912 that preparations were made for another flight across the Irish Sea, by Vivian Hewitt, a brewer from North Wales. Early in 1912, though he had not yet achieved his Aviator's Certificate, Hewitt took delivery of a new Gnome-powered Blériot monoplane at Brooklands. He transported it to Foryd aerodrome, near Abergele in North Wales, where he began a series of well-publicised flights. They were not uneventful, for on 25 February he experienced engine failure at 100 feet, just after take-off, and crashed through a fence, though without harm to himself.

In April Hewitt announced his intention of making the first flight from Holyhead to Dublin. He waited at Rhyl for favourable weather, but his attempt was forestalled by another, impromptu, flight.

Two Irish aviators, D Corbett-Wilson and Damar Leslie Allen, suddenly decided to attempt the flight to their homeland, and set off from Hendon in their Blériot monoplanes on 17 April. Corbett-Wilson had learned to fly at the Blériot School at Pau, making at least one notable flight, from Pau to Lourdes and back, during January 1912. Allen learned to fly at the Blériot School at Hendon, and on 20 February 1912 was awarded Aviator's Certificate No. 183.

Surprisingly, it was apparently without a wager that the two Irishmen set off, just after 3.30 pm

3. D. Corbett-Wilson, the first man to fly from Great Britain to Ireland – all the way.

on 17 April, each going their own way. Allen flew along the London & Northwestern Railway line, but became lost 10 miles beyond Crewe, and had to land to discover his whereabouts. He flew on and landed at Chester at about 6.30 pm. Corbett-Wilson took a route towards South Wales, and landed that evening at Almeley, 15 miles north of Hereford.

Just after 6 am on 18 April Allen took off from Chester, and was seen passing over Holyhead about an hour later. He was never seen again. No trace of him or his aircraft has ever been found.

Corbett-Wilson took off from Almeley at 4.30 pm on the 18 April, but was forced to land at Colva, Radnorshire, with engine trouble. It was not until Sunday 21 April, that he was able to continue, taking off early in the morning and flying to Fishguard. Early on the 22nd he took off again, heading for Wexford across the St George's Channel. The crossing to Ireland took him one hour and forty minutes, and he landed at Crane, 2 miles from Enniscorthy.

This was the first time that the flight from Great Britain to Ireland had been made entirely by air, without the pilot getting his feet wet. However, Vivian Hewitt was quick to point out that the St George's Channel was no more the Irish Sea than the English Channel was the North Sea, and went ahead with preparations for his own flight.

He had left Rhyl at 5 am on Sunday 21 April, heading for Holyhead, but was forced to land at Plas on Anglesey after a flight of one hour and twenty minutes. He flew at 5000 feet, and could see beyond Snowdon in one direction, and Holyhead Harbour in another. He suffered severe turbulence,

4. **(Above) Vivian Hewitt about to make his flight to Ireland, a still from a silent movie made at the time.**

5. **(Left) Vivian Hewitt in his Blériot monoplane, the first man to fly the Irish Sea.**

struggling against a wind that threatened to blow him out to sea, and had to dive towards the coast with the throttle wide open in order to make land. He managed to land at Plas at 6.20 am, feeling quite ill. The next morning he flew on to Lord Sheffield's field at Penhros Park, Robert Loraine's starting point nearly two years before.

Though this flight took only twenty minutes he was unable to continue because of dense sea-fog. He was then kept on the ground until Friday by strong winds blowing in the wrong direction. At 10.30 am on 26 April he set off for Ireland, his take-off being filmed by one of the silent movie cameras of the day. Like Loraine, he had equipped himself with a safety belt, and all shipping on the route had been asked to look out for him.

After ten minutes he lost sight of land in the haze, but five minutes after that he flew right over the packet boat from Kingstown, losing sight of it again within three minutes. Such was the height he was flying that none of the ships along his route saw him passing, and he saw nothing more for fifty minutes. He steered by the sun, but at times flew into dense banks of fog, and could not even see his wing tips. After just over an hour and ten minutes he saw the distant Wicklow Mountains, and soon passed over Kingstown Harbour.

He flew over Dublin at 2000 feet and began to descend towards Phoenix Park. In an echo of Loraine's flight he began to experience violent turbulence, and at one point the Blériot dropped like a stone for 500 feet Unlike Loraine, however, he made a safe landing, in Phoenix Park, claiming to be the first man to fly the Irish Sea.

On 1 August 1912 Rhyl Urban District Council, in a ceremony in the Marine Gardens, presented him with a silver cup in honour of his achievement, but there is little else in the way of recognition. Hewitt's flight was even greeted with humour at Hendon, where it was recalled that on his first flight in his Blériot he had climbed to 1000 feet, but had a righteous horror of banking, and so found turning difficult. By slight movements of the rudder he managed to get the aircraft pointed back at the airfield after having travelled about 15 miles, and then made a good landing after gliding down from 1500 feet. It was suggested that he had had to fly to Ireland, because having taken off from Holyhead, he could not turn round to come back again!

In a curious footnote to the Irish Sea flights, Robert Loraine volunteered for the Royal Flying Corps at the outset of the War, but after crashing two of the Service's precious few aircraft was made an observer, one of the first handful that served in France. In November 1915 he was badly wounded while spotting for the guns over the front line. His pilot for that flight was D Corbett-Wilson, the second man to fly to Ireland. After recovering from his wounds, Loraine took pilot training and eventually rose to command No. 40 Squadron, and then No. 17 Wing.

The *Guinness Book of Air Facts and Feats* lists Robert Loraine as the first man to have flown the Irish Sea, with no mention of Corbett-Wilson or Hewitt. Perhaps the one clear fact in the affair is that Loraine did not fly the Irish Sea, any more than Hubert Latham first flew the English Channel – they both got their feet wet. D Corbett-Wilson was the first man to fly from Great Britain to Ireland (all the way), on 22 April 1912, but as he traversed the St George's Channel, Vivian Hewitt was indeed the first to fly the Irish Sea.

The residents of the farthest corner of Anglesey, are now more used to aviation, with RAF Valley's Hawks always overhead – so different from those few weeks in 1910 when Robert Loraine visited them, after force-landing in their midst.

CHAPTER 2

Down on the Railway

When aircraft have suffered engine trouble in hilly or forested regions, pilots have often resorted to putting their aircraft down on roads, sometimes the only available piece of cleared or level land. When that road is a railroad, it not only results in a bumpy touchdown, but if a train is coming, a situation worthy of a Buster Keaton film can result.

In 1910 Captain George William Patrick Dawes was a serving officer in the British Army. He had served with distinction in the Boer War, where the Army had used tethered balloons for observation purposes. Intrigued by the new science of heavier-than-air flight he resolved to learn to fly himself. He bought a Blériot Monoplane and had it shipped to Dunstall Park Racecourse, Wolverhampton.

Dunstall Park had just been offered to the newly formed Midland Aero Club for use as their airfield. As such, it was one of the few dedicated airfields in Great Britain, though it was understood that race meetings would always take precedence over the needs of the aviators. The Midland Aero Club had announced the first All-British Flying Meeting, to take place at Dunstall Park during the week commencing 27 June 1910.

There had been two flying meetings in Britain during 1909, at Doncaster and Blackpool, but they had largely been dominated by French flyers. This, the third meeting overall, would be restricted to British pilots possessing an Aviator's Certificate, issued in any country. The Midland Aero Club erected a row of six wooden hangars on one side of the racecourse, and flyers began to arrive about three weeks before the meeting was due to start. Among them were a number who had not yet qualified for the Aviator's Certificate, but hoped to do so before the Flying Meeting.

One of the aircraft was a Star Monoplane, built in Wolverhampton, and to be flown by its designer Granville Eastwood Bradshaw. Another was a Humber Monoplane, a Blériot built under licence by Humber Cars in Coventry, entered by Mr N Holder of Edgbaston, Birmingham. There was also Captain Dawes and his Blériot.

By 8 June he had his aircraft erected and took it up for his first tentative hops, to a height of about 20 to 25 feet. He did not attempt a turn as yet, something he would need to learn quite quickly on what was quite a restricted airfield. The racecourse was triangular in shape, each side being roughly 6 furlongs. There was open country on two sides, but on the third the ground rose quite steeply to Oxley Railway Sidings, with a viaduct of over 100 feet right behind the hangars. Later, more experienced pilots arrived and made the Committee change the shape of the course so that it was four sided, reducing the tightness of the turns required.

On the following day Dawes tried a few more hops, much appreciated by the crowds that were already gathering in their hundreds each day. On the 10 June Holder brought out his Humber Monoplane, and he, too, tried a few hops of 10 to 15 feet in height, the crowd giving him a burst of applause for his efforts. The following morning Dawes made his most ambitious flight to date. He managed to circle the racecourse twice, and repeated the feat after breakfast. Such early morning flights were usual, because the wind was often less strong in the early hours. Dawes' turns were rather flat, skidding affairs, as the necessity for banking was not yet generally understood.

By now Granville Bradshaw had brought out the Star Monoplane, and he was attempting low hops, along with Holder, but it was Dawes who continued to be the star of the show. Two days later he was reported to have 'surprised and surpassed himself' with an inadvertent cross-country flight. The country he had inadvertently crossed was reported with due reverence in the local paper as being 'some trees, a fence, and part of an adjoining field'. He had intended to fly around some trees and a house at the western

6. Captain George William Patrick Dawes, surveying the wreck of his Blériot Monoplane at Dunstall Park, Wolverhampton, on 17 June 1910, the same aircraft he was to force-land on the Bombay-to-Baroda railway line.

end of the course, but had gone too far and ended up landing in an adjoining field.

On 17 June Captain Dawes came to grief. He twice circled the racecourse, reaching a height of about 100 feet. As he approached the hangars he swooped down to within a few feet of the ground, and then pulled the Blériot up into a steep climb. Undoubtedly, he stalled the aircraft, which plummeted to the ground. It landed on its side, smashing one wing, the propeller and the undercarriage. Luckily, Dawes stepped out unhurt from the wreck. Wood and fabric aircraft were very good at absorbing the shock of an impact as they crumpled up.

The crash had put paid to any chance Dawes had of entering the Flying Meeting. The Blériot was repaired and after the Meeting, on 26 July, he gained his Aviator's Certificate at Dunstall Park. It was only the seventeenth such certificate issued in Great Britain. Eleven of the other certificate holders had taken part in the Meeting, together with two or three others who held French certificates.

Captain Dawes was posted to India after his adventures in Wolverhampton and took his Blériot Monoplane with him. He was credited with making the first ever flight on the Indian subcontinent, and was then to survive an extraordinary forced landing. On 26 March 1911 he was flying to the north of Bombay when the Anzani engine of the Blériot stopped. He quickly looked round for somewhere to land the aircraft, but there seemed to be nowhere flat enough and clear of trees and obstacles.

The Bombay-to-Baroda railway line was below, and he glided down to land on that. As he did so, he saw, to his horror, that there was a goods train approaching. The Blériot touched down and rolled bumpily to a halt in a few yards. The great snorting steam engine was almost upon him. Dawes scrambled frantically from the aircraft, jumping to the ground and then running clear. He turned round in time to see the engine smash into his beloved aircraft, pulverising it into splinters. By great fortune, he had escaped entirely uninjured, but the aircraft was wrecked beyond repair. This was not the end of his flying career however.

Dawes applied to join the Royal Flying Corps at its formation in 1912. In July he was one of the RFC observers at the Military Aircraft Competition held at Larkhill, to determine the best aircraft for the RFC to order; a competition won by the totally unsuitable Cody Biplane. He was posted to No. 2 Squadron and took part in their epic flight in their BE2as to Montrose, which was their assigned base.

No. 2 Squadron quickly became recognised as the RFC's premier squadron. In May 1914 the Squadron received orders to fly south to the RFC's concentration camp at Netheravon. Dawes flew one of the ten BE2as that took off, followed by thirty-four vehicles with the rest of the equipment and men. The squadron was sent to France at the outbreak of the First World War and Dawes received his first of seven Mentions in Dispatches on 8 October when he was attached to the Royal Berkshire Regiment.

By 1 January 1916 he was a temporary major in command of No. 29 Squadron. In this position he gave evidence to the Official Inquiry into the performance of the RFC and its aircraft during the first years of the First

World War, with particular reference to the events of 10 March. On this date No. 29 Squadron left Gosport for France, and six of the ten aircraft that took off suffered damage during forced landings because they flew into the middle of a snowstorm.

By 8 October 1916 Dawes was a temporary lieutenant-colonel in command of the RFC in the Balkans, where he served until 1918, rising in rank to an acting general. In addition to his seven Mentions in Dispatches in the First World War and the Queen's Medal with three clasps, and the King's Medal with two clasps awarded in the Boer War, he also received the DSO and the AFC. From grateful allies he received the *Croix de Guerre*, with three palms; the Serbian Order of the White Eagle; the Order of the Redeemer of Greece; and was created *Officer de Legion d'Honneur*.

In the Second World War Dawes served with the Royal Air Force as a wing commander, retiring in 1946 with the MBE. In addition to his impressive collection of medals he had the distinction of being one of the few men to serve in the Boer War and in the First and Second World Wars. He did so for three different services, the Army, the RFC and the RAF. He was probably the only man to be able to claim this honour.

Considering his adventurous life, among other things surviving his crash at Dunstall Park and his forced landing on a railway line, it is something of a wonder that he reached the ripe old age of eighty. He died in March 1960.

CHAPTER 3

Down in the Sahara

Deserts have claimed the lives of many aircrew even from the earliest days of aviation. The aircraft was quickly seen as a way of crossing the huge expanses of the world's deserts at a pace somewhat quicker than a camel. In the First World War in particular the use of aircraft quickly became essential. The aircraft of the day operated at a sufficiently slow speed for a forced landing to be a survivable event, but conversely the unreliability of the engines, made a forced landing a most likely event.

Second Lieutenant Stewart Gordon Ridley was the son of Mr TW Ridley of Willimoteswick, Redcar, but his mother was an Irishwoman from Derry. He was also a descendant of Bishop Ridley of Northumberland, one of the victims of Queen Mary, Bloody Mary, in the sixteenth century. He was educated at Mr J Roscoe's School at Harrogate, and then at Oundle, where he was in the Officer Cadet Corps for three years. He left school shortly before the War and was preparing to go into business, but enlisted in September 1914, along with his brother.

He became a private in the 4th Yorkshire Regiment, and in February 1915 received a commission in the 12th Yorkshire Regiment. He left that Regiment in July and joined the RFC, going to France as an observer in August 1915. He served on the Western Front for four months and then returned to the United Kingdom to take pilot training. On receiving his Pilot's Certificate he was posted to No. 17 Squadron in Egypt, still only 19 years of age.

No. 17 Squadron had been formed at Gosport in February 1915, and began to equip with the BE2c. Down the coast at Shoreham No. 14 Squadron was formed the same month, and though it initially received Maurice Farman Longhorns, was also to acquire BE2cs.

Both squadrons were shipped out to Alexandria in November 1915, where they made up No. 5 Wing, the aerial component of the Army in Egypt. They soon found themselves in action on three separate fronts. They directly faced the Turks in the Sinai; they operated in support of the Arab Revolt in Arabia, also against the Turks; and they faced an uprising by the Senussi in the Libyan Desert. The Libyan Desert did not just refer to that portion of the Sahara that lay within the borders of Libya, but referred generally to the desert west of the Nile.

The headquarters of No. 5 Wing was at Heliopolis, but the two squadrons operated flights as wide apart as Port Sudan on the Red Sea and Sidi

7. A No. 17 Squadron BE2c, somewhere in the Middle East, the type flown by Second Lieutenant Ridley on his last flight.

Barrani on the Mediterranean near the Egyptian/Libyan border. No. 17 Squadron in particular operated flights within Egypt at El Hammâm, Suez, Assiut, Meheriq, and Port Sudan, with brief detachments to airstrips all over the country.

The BE2c aircraft had, by now, begun to suffer a poor reputation on the Western Front, where its great stability, and low performance made it a not very agile opponent when faced with the new generation of fighter aircraft that were appearing. Its observer was sited in the front cockpit, between the wings and surrounded by a veritable birdcage of struts and bracing wires, so that aiming a gun at an attacker, no matter how ingenious the gun mounting, was almost an impossibility.

In the desert, however, its stability, low landing speed and relative robustness, made it an almost ideal support to the Camel Corps, as long as aerial opposition remained scarce. The engine was the Royal Aircraft Factory's version of the old 70 hp air-cooled Renault V8, which had equipped early versions. The RAF1a engine gave an extra 20 hp over the old Renault, giving the aircraft a moderate absolute top speed of 86 mph at sea level. The RAF1a engine did not take kindly to running on maximum rpm for very long, however, and cooling of the rear pair of cylinders was always marginal. A curved air scoop was fitted over the engine to help channel air to the rear. The immense heat of the Sahara desert in the summer months only made the problem worse.

On 16 April two aircraft of No. 17 Squadron's flight at Assiut, on the Nile about halfway between Cairo and Aswan, were moved to Meheriq in the Kharga Oasis, a large oasis around 180 miles west of the Nile. In June Second Lieutenant Stewart Ridley, more usually know as 'Riddles' to his RFC colleagues, arrived in Egypt, and was sent straight down to Meheriq to join this isolated detachment. The hot, dry weather of the Sahara must have had a severe impact on a lad more used to the bracing winds of the north-eastern coasts of England.

On 15 June, which was a Thursday, he was detailed to fly a BE2c solo as escort to another aircraft, flown by a pilot named Gardiner, with a mechanic named JA Garside in the observer's seat. Gardiner and Garside were going to a new airstrip about 60 miles to the west at a small oasis; the airstrip had been prepared by a patrol of the Imperial Camel Corps, which had travelled out there some days earlier.

They left in the afternoon, and flew steadily west in loose formation. The airstrip should have been about an hour's flying time from Meheriq, but as time passed by there was still no sign of it, though the shadows of the camel patrol would have been long in the setting sun. After an hour and a half it was beginning to get dark as the sun dropped below the horizon ahead of them, so Gardiner signalled that they should land.

He chose a suitably flat-looking spot in the gravel desert, and brought his BE2c in for a reasonable landing. When Ridley saw that Gardiner was down safely, he followed. They set up camp for the night, having brought food and water, as a natural precaution. The Saharan night was cold, but there was nothing with which they could light a fire, so they had to keep warm as well as they could.

They awoke to an inclement morning, and Ridley suggested that he should take off solo and try and find the tracks of the camel patrol, returning to them when successful. Garside swung the four-blade propeller of the BE2c, but the engine would not start. It had been running roughly the previous afternoon.

Gardiner decided that he should fly solo back to Meheriq, to find the exact location of the new airstrip. He would return the following morning, which would be Saturday 17 June. He left all the remaining water and food with Ridley and Garside, and took off. When he landed back at Meheriq he found the Camel Corps Patrol already there. When the aviators had not arrived on the Thursday they had returned to find out what was happening. The captain of the patrol climbed into Gardiner's BE2c and flew with him to the new airstrip.

The following morning they set off for the site of the forced landing. When they found the site, with some difficulty, they found Ridley's aircraft had gone. Gardiner landed in the hope that some sort of note had been left, but though there were odds and ends lying about there was no sign of a note. They took off again and flew back to Meheriq, fully expecting to find Ridley and Garside waiting for them there, having flown back when they got the recalcitrant engine going, but there was no news of them.

An immediate search was organised with camel patrols, motorcars and aircraft setting off to scour the desert between the two airstrips. The patrols found nothing until the following day. On the afternoon of Sunday 18 June, a pilot found signs of another forced landing in the desert, about 25 miles from the first one. The pilot landed and confirmed that the other BE2c had been there. Repairs had apparently been made to the aircraft, before they had flown on.

The search continued but they began to give up hope when the tracks of two men walking were discovered; these tracks were joined and followed by another set of tracks, the tracks of several camels. It was feared that a group of Senussi had followed the two men, but whether they might have killed or captured them was a matter for conjecture.

On the afternoon of Tuesday 20 June a motor patrol finally saw Ridley's BE2c standing in the desert. As they drove nearer they could see two men lying on the ground, one beneath the shade of the aircraft's wing, one lying some way away in the burning sun. As the cars drove up there was no sign of movement from the two figures.

The cars stopped, and the engines were switched off, but there was still no movement from the figures. As the searchers approached the man lying in the sun, it was immediately clear why he was not moving. The sickly smell and the gathering flies would have been enough to tell them he was dead. It was Ridley, and it was obvious that he had been shot in the head. His service revolver was in his hand. It was Garside lying in the shade of the wing, and he too was dead, though with no apparent marks on him. It was suspected that he had just died of thirst, waiting for the rescue which had come too late.

Luckily, Garside had left a short scribbled diary, which explained what had happened when Gardiner had left them in the desert. After the other BE2c had flown away they had worked on the engine, and managed to get it going. Garside quickly threw everything they needed into the aircraft, with the propeller blowing up a cloud of dust, and then he clambered into the front cockpit. Ridley took off, but after flying for 25 minutes the engine stopped once more and Ridley brought it down for a second forced landing in the desert.

Garside once more began to tinker with the engine, but did not manage to get it going until the following day, which was the Saturday. Working on an engine in the full heat of the mid-summer sun in the Sahara desert, is not easy. Metal becomes too hot to touch, spanners left lying in the sun will burn the hand that picks them up. Nevertheless, Garside managed once more to breath life into the stubborn engine. Again Ridley took off, but this time the engine stopped after they had only gone about 5 miles, and they made a third forced landing.

They spent another cold night in the desert, and then all through Sunday morning they tried to get the engine going again. However, swinging the big propeller was not easy, and Garside was soon sweating profusely. He was getting weaker and weaker and using up his precious bodily fluids far too quickly, and there was only about half a bottle of water left. Ridley suggested they walk to a line of low hills they could see not too far away, where they might have a good vantage point to spot searching parties.

They began the walk across the desert, the only sound the crunch of their boots on the gravel. In the unusual perspectives of the desert the hills were much further away than they had seemed, and by the time that the two men arrived at their summit, they were both exhausted. They stared around the naked horizon, but there was nothing to see, except their own aircraft, a tiny insignificant toy in the vast emptiness.

Deflated, they began the weary walk back to the aircraft. By the time they collapsed to the ground under the shade of the wing it was beginning to get dark, with the suddeness that was usual in the desert. Ridley was totally despondent. Their thirst was overpowering, they were exhausted, and rescue seemed further away than ever.

At about 10.30 pm, when Garside's back was turned, Ridley took his service revolver and shot himself in the head. As the sudden shot cracked the silence of the night, Garside spun round, but there was nothing he could do. Though it would be suggested that Ridley had shot himself so that his companion would have a better chance of survival, there was only a drop of water left; his death would make little difference. Despair was the most likely explanation; the despair of a man who had only been in the desert for a few days, who had not acclimatised to its fierce heat, and its vast loneliness.

The following day, Monday, 19 June Garside just lay in the shade of the wing, conserving what little strength and bodily fluid he had left. He did think of the water in the aircraft's compass. He managed to get about half a pint of fluid from it, and drank it though he found it was some kind of spirit. He fired four rounds from the Lewis gun, but that attracted no attention. That night he fired the last cartridges of the Very pistol. They arced forlornly into the desert sky, but brought no help. His last entry in his makeshift diary read 'Could last days, if had water'.

The two men were buried on the spot beneath a heap of stones. The following Sunday, 25 June, a chaplain came out and conducted a service over the graves, and then two crosses were erected in that lonely place.

Only a week later, on 2 July 1916, No. 17 Squadron sailed from Alexandria *en route* for Salonika, to take the war against the Turks into the Balkans. They left behind a mute memorial to four days of suffering for two young Englishmen far from home, isolated graves probably never visited again, and all but forgotten. It would not be the last time a forced landing in the Libyan Desert would claim the lives of an aircrew as they waited in vain for rescue.

CHAPTER 4

Down on Lake Tanganyika

In 1915 the Belgians fought a very private and isolated war with the Germans across the waters of Lake Tanganyika. Four Short seaplanes supplied by the British played an integral part of this little war. These aircraft pioneered military aviation in the heart of Africa, where any kind of modern facilities were non-existent, and where a forced landing was liable to be in the most inhospitable of places.

At the beginning of the First World War the Dark Continent had seen very little of the aeroplane, but the requirements of war, and the vast distances between the belligerent armies in Africa, soon led to their introduction. The bulk of Africa was largely carved up between five European nations: Great Britain, France, Germany, Portugal and Belgium. The colonists lost no time in following their home nations into the War and the German colonies of Tanganyika, South West Africa and Cameroon found themselves with enemies on all sides.

The Germans in Western Tanganyika were very swift to organise belligerent action. On 15 August 1914, only the day after war was declared, they launched an attack by boat across Lake Tanganyika on the Belgian Congo village of Mokobolu. A few days later they struck again, this time against the larger town of Lukuga (later to be renamed Albertville, and now known as Kalémié).

The Belgians were completely unprepared to defend the vast territory of the Congo, and only had a few companies of soldiers and a handful of artillery pieces. Communications between garrisons were often reliant on native runners, as telegraph wires did not survive long in the jungle, and roads were practically non-existent. The River Congo was the main artery of communication, but away from that communities were very isolated.

Worse was to come after the Germans salvaged some guns from the heavy cruiser *Konigsberg* which was sunk by the British in the Rufiji Delta. These were fitted to a couple of large steamers, which had previously plied the waters of the Lake on purely peaceful purposes, the *Graf von Goetzen* and the *Hedwig von Wisman*. These ships proceeded to shell the Belgian garrisons on the west bank of the Lake with impunity.

As well as these two powerful ships, which were based at Kigoma (the western terminus of the railway across Tanganyika and the main German port on the Lake), the Germans had two smaller gunboats, the *Wami* and the *Kingani*. In opposition the commander of the Belgian forces, General Tombeur, fitted out a small steamer, the *Netta*, and a trawler, the *Vengeur*, with a couple of old three-inch guns, and also had two smaller armed boats. The British had nothing on the Lake, though they occupied the southern shoreline in Northern Rhodesia. They transported two armed launches, the *Mimi* and the *Toutou*, from England, setting out from the Thames on 15 May 1915. They were shipped to Cape Town and then transported by rail as far as Fungurumee, the nearest point to the Lake on the Rhodesian Railway. From there they were hauled by steam traction engine many miles overland to the Lake, where they were operated by twenty-seven officers and men.

On 6 March 1915 General Tombeur sent a detailed report to Belgium complaining that there was little that he could do with the facilities at his disposal. He suggested that some aircraft might at least have a reconnaissance role to play, furnishing him with details of where the Germans actually were. The Belgian Air Force had few aircraft on the Western Front, and none of those were suitable for conversion to seaplanes for operating on Lake Tanganyika. The Belgiums asked for help from the British Admiralty, who offered to supply them with four Short Type 827 seaplanes, which had been shipped out to No. 8 Squadron, operating from Zanzibar.

The Short Type 827 was a two-seat biplane with an upper span of 53 feet, 11 inches and a length of 35 feet, 3 inches. It was powered by a 150 hp Sunbeam Crusader V8 side-valve engine, which gave it a maximum speed of 62 mph and a duration of 3.5 hours. Three of the four aircraft concerned (3093, 3094, and 3095) were actually the first three built by the Sunbeam Motor Car Co. in Wolverhampton, the first three of forty they were to build, fitting their own V8 Crusader engines.

The three seaplanes had all been delivered to RNAS Grain in November 1915, before passing on to Short's at Rochester for testing. They then went to RNAS Westgate for onward shipment to East Africa aboard the seaplane carrier, *Laconia*, along with a fourth example, serial 8219, which had been built by Parnall & Sons at Bristol. When the *Laconia* arrived in East Africa the seaplanes were operated from Chukwani Bay.

The four seaplanes were reassigned to the Belgians, crated and transported round to the mouth of the River Congo, and then up the river, before being transported overland to Lukuga. The Belgian air and ground crew assigned to operate the four seaplanes travelled out from Europe. The crews for the seaplanes had been selected from volunteers on the Western Front, of which there was no shortage.

The detachment, which left Europe on New Year's Day 1916, was commanded by Commandant de Bueger, and included three pilots, Lieutenants Orta, Behaeghe and Castiau, and as observers,

8. One of the Short 827s destined for the Belgian Congo, under construction in the Sunbeam factory in Wolverhampton.

Lieutenants Colignon and Ruschaert. There were also two mechanics and two carpenters. They arrived at the mouth of the Congo on 4 February, and went up river to a point where they could trek overland to Lukuga.

Once by the Lake it was clear that its vast size made it more an inland sea than the calm lake they had expected, with very strong prevailing winds and waves to match. It was clear that operating the Short 827s from the main lake would be a hazardous business, except on the few days when sufficiently calm conditions prevailed, and they began looking for a more suitable place. North of Lukuga they discovered a small side lake, named Tongwe, near the village of M'Toa.

The Navy loaded the seaplanes and about 500 tons of equipment that were now at Lukuga and transported them up the coast. The Belgian Army established a defensive ring around the new base. They then set the natives to work digging a short canal to link the two lakes. In the event this was never finished, as the earth proved too soft, and there were frequent land slips. All the equipment therefore had to be hauled overland from Lake Tanganyika to M'Toa.

They also had to construct huts to house themselves and their equipment, which included 10,000 gallons of petrol, 500 gallons of oil, 250 No. 65 lb bombs, 750 No. 16 lb bombs, four machine-guns and about 30,000 rounds of ammunition. The four seaplanes came in eight crates, and there were also a few spare parts and two spare engines. These were essential

9. Short 827s being assembled at M'Toa on the banks of Lake Tongwe.

10. Short 827 No. 8219 at M'Toa. This was the sole Parnall-built aircraft of the four.

for the early Sunbeam side-valve engines, which were not very reliable. The valves tended to run hot, and then distorted on cooling. Wherever possible, mechanics would change an engine after each flight.

While the laborious process of establishing an air force on the Lake was taking place, the Allied naval forces there achieved a major success. On 9 February a joint British and Belgian force found and attacked the *Hedwig von Wisman* and destroyed it. This was only a few days after the British launches had captured another German steamer, the *Kingani*. There only remained the *Graf von Goetzen*, but that was easily the most powerful warship on the Lake.

By 13 May the first seaplane was ready to fly, and the following day Lieutenant Orta took it up on its first test flight. It was also his first flight in a Short Type 827, or any kind of seaplane, as there had been no time to find one to practice with before leaving Europe. The second seaplane was ready on 24 May and an operation against the *Graf von Goetzen* was planned with all haste.

Commandant de Bueger had the use of the armed trawler *Vengeur*, and the Belgian launches *Mimi* and *Toutou*, as well as the British launch *Fifi*. Kigoma was 165 miles away on the other side of the Lake to the north-east, and de Bueger planned to station the *Vengeur* about halfway across the lake in case of engine trouble. Lieutenant Orta was to make the attack in the first of the seaplanes, but unfortunately the next day he experienced engine trouble on a test flight and damaged his aircraft landing on Lake Tongwe, which was rather rough that day.

Lieutenant Behaeghe was assigned to fly the bombing attack in the second aircraft, on 6 June, but there was no wind and the heavily laden seaplane refused to leave the water. It was only in the evening of the 7th that the wind became suitable and the *Vengeur* was sent steaming into position.

11. Local labour launching one of the Short 827s into the Lake.

Behaeghe and his observer Lieutenant Colignon took off at 6 pm and set course, carrying two 65 lb bombs. They were almost in sight of the German base when the engine began to run rough. Behaeghe turned away and nursed his failing Sunbeam Crusader, but eventually had to land on the Lake, about 20 miles from Kigoma. Two hours later the *Vengeur* appeared and took them in tow. The long slow tow ended at 7 am next day when they emerged from the mist off the village of M'Toa.

By 10 June Orta's aircraft had been repaired and it was bombed up for another attempt to attack the *Graf von Goetzen*. With Lieutenant Ruschaert as his observer he took off at about 6 pm. In the Short Type 827 the pilot sat in the rear seat and the observer had a cockpit over the centre of gravity between the wings. In typical Short Bros' fashion there was a large radiator block on top of the forward fuselage, which from most angles looked as if it would block their forward vision, but it was in fact made up of four vertical panels, through which they could see straight ahead perfectly well. Through this radiator they could soon see the dark outline of the eastern shore of the Lake.

Ten miles from Kigoma, Orta descended to about 500 feet, planning to make a low-level attack on the warship, to ensure that his two small bombs had every chance of striking home. He was still two miles out when the Germans heard him coming. Despite the shock of discovering that the enemy had an aircraft operating on the Lake, the gunners on the ship and the shore began opening fire.

It was a long two minutes as the little seaplane roared towards the harbour and over the ship, and the Short began to take a number of hits, but neither Orta or his observer were wounded. As he flashed over the gunboat he dropped his two 65 lb bombs and zoomed away, straining his neck round to see where they landed. One of the bombs exploded on the stern of the ship and one fell ten yards short.

Elated by their successful attack, Orta set course for M'Toa, but about 20 miles out over the Lake the Sunbeam engine began misfiring. He nursed it as best he could but it continued to cough and splutter, and the aircraft lost height quickly. Eventually, he had to bring it in for a landing on the choppy waters. The floats had been hit during the attack, and they began to take on water. The little seaplane began sinking slowly, and having no safety equipment there was nothing Orta and Ruschaert could do but sit there in the darkness as the Short bobbed about lower and lower on the Lake.

Only the wooden construction of the aircraft saved them, remaining buoyant enough to keep it from sinking. They were in the centre of Africa, 20 miles from the nearest shore of a lake swept clear of the normal ships of commerce by the tides of war. There was no way they could save themselves; they just had to sit and wait in the darkness, and hope the *Vengeur* came in time.

Once they were overdue the captain of the armed trawler set course for Kigoma, as he had for Behaeghe in the earlier raid. Eventually, he found the stricken seaplane and saved its desperate crew. The aircraft too was salvaged, and they arrived back at M'Toa twenty hours later.

The *Graf von Goetzen* had been badly damaged, but the Germans' discovery that the Allies had aircraft on the Lake was a greater shock. Fearing that the bombing attack presaged a large operation, they pulled in some of their outlying garrisons, bringing relief to the hard pressed and scattered Belgians.

A brigade was organised to move round the Lake to attack Kigoma from the South and on 9 July Orta flew a reconnaissance mission over the town, his observer taking several photographs. These revealed that not only was the *Graf von Goetzen* still afloat, but the Germans were arming another steamer as a warship.

Commandant de Bueger decided to attack the town with a force of three of the seaplanes. They took off on the 12 July, but found mist obscuring the eastern side of the Lake and could not find Kigoma, and flew back to M'Toa. On landing back on Lake Tongwe Lieutenant Castiau crashed the third seaplane. As there were only three pilots the fourth seaplane had been left in its crates, and de Bueger postponed another attack on Kigoma until that was ready.

Meanwhile the other two seaplanes flew a series of bombing and reconnaissance missions against other targets around the Lake. On 23 July the two aircraft returned to the attack against Kigoma, and bombed the town from 300 feet. The *Graf von Goetzen* had been stripped of all armament, and the conversion of the other steamer had ceased. Three days later the Belgian Brigade marching up from the south launched an attack on the town, but Kigoma surrendered without a shot being fired. All the shoreline of Lake Tanganyika was in Allied hands.

On 18 August the three Belgian pilots flew their aircraft to Kigoma and landed in the harbour they had previously attacked. For several days they flew demonstration flights, to impress the natives and entertain the troops. The seaplanes were no longer needed in the continuing war against the Germans in Tanganyika, which continued into 1918, and were returned to the RNAS, No. 8219 at least surviving until 1918. The air and ground crew were sent back to Europe, where they were to operate French Schreck FBA flying boats from Calais for the rest of the war.

The four seaplanes had brought aviation to that part of Africa for the first time, and they had conducted a successful military operation without major loss. Twice, aircraft had force-landed in the middle of the Lake, and twice successful planning had saved both aircraft and crew.

CHAPTER 5

Down on the Ice Pack

Today an aircraft forced landing on the ice packs of the North Pole would still leave its crew in real peril. Even with satellite navigation systems and communications, the weather in the Arctic might well make rescue impossible for days, even using long-range helicopters. In the 1920s the crew of any aircraft forced down on the ice were usually left with only one option, to save themselves.

During the middle and late 1920s, with many of the oceans of the world having been conquered by the aeroplane, a number of people began to turn their attention to the challenge of a flight over the Arctic Sea, and over the North Pole. The Norwegian Roald Amundsen had been the leader of the first expedition to visit the South Pole. He had spent a quarter of a century on polar exploration, with notable expeditions looking for the North-West Passage and the North-East Passage, a seven-year odyssey by his ship *Maud,* which he was to leave to make an attempt to fly to the North Pole.

It was perhaps inevitable that he would be one of the first to take an interest in using aircraft to explore the polar regions. He had obtained the very first Norwegian civilian pilot's licence in 1914, which opened his eyes to the speed of transit compared to the tortuous journey to the South Pole he had made with his dog-sled teams. He also knew the advantages of high altitude in any exploration.

In 1923 he had a trial flight in Alaska in a Junkers monoplane, but he was unsure at the time whether it would be better to use an aeroplane or an airship. He decided initially to use two Dornier Wal flying boats, and placed an order for them despite the fact that his personal finances were in a shocking state and he had just declared himself bankrupt. He journeyed to America to try to raise funds with lectures and other means, but without a great degree of success. Luckily, a rich American named

12. Roald Amundsen, the veteran Norwegian explorer.

Lincoln Ellsworth came to his assistance. Ellsworth was a young man who had tried to persuade his father to finance an Arctic expedition of his own, but his father would not trust his son in the Arctic wilderness. However with an experienced man like Amundsen in charge he was prepared to relent. Ellsworth Snr. financed the expedition and the purchase of the aircraft, which were serialled N24 and N25, each powered by two 370 hp Rolls-Royce Eagle engines. Lincoln Ellsworth was happy to play a subordinate role and to allow the expedition to operate under the Norwegian flag.

On 15 April 1925 the two aircraft were landed at King's Bay, Svalbard. The flight to the North Pole began on 21 May with Norwegian pilots for each aircraft, Hjalmar Riiser-Larsen in N25 with Amundsen as navigator and a German mechanic, Carl Feucht, and Lief Dietrichson in N24 with Ellsworth as navigator and Norwegian Oskar Omdahl as mechanic. The normal maximum load of the Wal was two and a half tons, but N25 carried half a ton more than this. N24 was damaged slightly during the take-off, but they decided to press on.

Take-off was at 17.00 hrs and for the first part of the journey they flew above a layer of fog, having climbed to 3000 feet to be clear of it. After two hours there was a break in the grey expanse and they could see the ice pack below them. Despite expecting the ice to be smooth enough to land the Dorniers if need be, they could see that the ice was very broken up and not at all suitable for landing; but confident in the reliability of their Rolls-Royce engines they pressed on.

Given the difficulty of navigating in a region where at the Pole itself every direction is south, at about 20.00 hrs, they were able to decide, by using their sun compass, that they were west of their preferred track. By 1 am on 22 May they had reached latitude 87 degrees 43 minutes. Then N25 began to have trouble with one of its engines, which was misfiring. Riiser-Larsen happily saw a clear strip on the ice pack and managed to bring the aircraft down in a neat forced landing. Dietrichson brought the second Wal down for a landing alongside his compatriot, but was not so successful and landed away from the clear strip, damaging the aircraft.

The crew members scrambled unhurt from the wreckage of N24 and made their way to N25. They were able to work out their position exactly, and decided they were only 136 miles from the Pole. The six men then began the arduous task of salvaging the remaining petrol from N24 and carrying it across the ice to N25. They had only the scantiest supplies, and no communication with the outside world, as at the last moment before the flight the radio equipment had been discarded in favour of more fuel. Fighting for survival against the Arctic weather, they struggled to solve the misfiring problem of the Rolls-Royce Eagle in N25, and then had to create a runway for take-off as there was not enough room on the small strip.

They had to clear a runway about a mile long, and wide enough for the wing tips to clear the jagged points of ice forced up on all sides. The only available tools they had were two small axes, three small knives which they lashed to ski poles, a boy scout hatchet and a camera tripod. After nearly clearing and levelling a strip long enough, the ice moved and the pressure cracked up the surface into a jagged maze once more. They were forced to start again from scratch.

For a second and third time they cleared runways, across the ice, almost starving from the lack of sustenance, combined with the arduous work in the cold climate. Each time the ice moved again, ruining their efforts. They then dragged the Wal to another point and started again, but once more when they had nearly finished the new runway, the ice moved. This time the ice threatened to close in and crush the hull of the flying boat itself. Omdahl, the only member of the party wearing rubber boots, jumped on and broke off the jagged points of ice as they threatened to pierce the thin metal skin of the hull, piling them under the aircraft. He continued to do this for hours until the broken ice that had been pushed underneath lifted the flying boat above the walls of ice that were closing inwards.

Back in Norway, search efforts had been organised to try and find the missing aircraft. Two ships, *Hobby* and *Fram* patrolled the edge of the ice barrier, and the Government began to organise the dispatch of two naval seaplanes to the North Cape. A French vessel, the *Pourquoi Pas,* was placed at the disposal of the search organisers by its commander Dr Charcot, while in America the Macmillan Expedition offered to assist in the search with its aircraft.

For a fifth time the six men lost on the ice moved N25 to a new situation and began a runway, but this too was destroyed by the movement of the ice. Finally, they began their sixth and last runway, and this time they had good luck. They trampled down soft snow which had fallen, and the snow froze to create a smooth slippery runway. They all climbed aboard the Wal and started the engines. They had lightened the aircraft by throwing off everything that was not essential to the flight back to Svalbard. The hull slid easily over the slippery ice and the aircraft lifted off. They had spent three weeks stranded on the ice, knowing that rescue was unlikely to come, and that therefore salvation was in their own hands. They set course for Svalbard and were very glad to reach it without further distress.

As they were approaching the North Cape of the island, after 8 hours 35 minutes flying, Dietrichson began to have trouble with the ailerons, and then one jammed. Dietrichson managed to make a safe landing on the squally sea, near to a sealing vessel, and soon they were safely on board it. The vessel was the *Sjoeliv* and it attempted to take the Dornier in tow, but a gale was beginning to blow up. The flying boat was therefore moored against the land-ice, and the crew were transported to King's Bay.

When the weather improved, Amundsen's vessel *Heimdal* took the two pilots and mechanics back to N25 and they flew it safely back to King's Bay. The other Wal, N24, was left on the Arctic ice pack, above an area where the sea bottom was believed to be 12,300 feet.

Amundsen and his men had been forced down in one of the most inhospitable places on the planet. By their own efforts they had survived, but he knew how close it had been. He had become very impressed at the dangers of using a heavier than air aircraft for polar flying. The absence of suitable places to land in the event of engine failure was obvious, but another peril was fog. The airship offered the simple expedient of hovering until fog cleared, and in the event of engine failure, it was often possible to repair it in the air. As soon as he reached civilisation, Amundesn established contact with General Umberto Nobile, the Italian airship constructor, and began negotiations for the purchase of his airship N1.

This airship was of the semi-rigid type, that is an envelope strengthened by a keel. Built in 1923, she was 348 feet long with a gas capacity of 672,000 cubic feet, and was powered by three 260 hp Maybach engines. It was soon apparent that the Italian Government, with the full support of Mussolini, was prepared to sell the N1 to Amundsen, and his colleague Riiser-Larsen went to Rome to negotiate. Amundsen went to America to raise money by lectures and other means, and his friend Lincoln Ellsworth continued to support him.

World interest was heightened when it became known that the American aviators Richard Evelyn Byrd and Floyd Bennett were making preparations for a flight from Svalbard to the North Pole and back in a Fokker Monoplane.

Special alterations were made to the airship N1, and it was renamed *Norge*. Nobile was made commander but a Norwegian crew was sent to Italy to be trained to fly it. Ellsworth had contributed about $25,000 towards the cost of purchasing the airship.

Norge was ready for her first test flight on 27 February 1926, and further trials went on into March. On 26 March Amundesn and Ellsworth arrived in Rome, and three days later *Norge* was formally handed over to them. Amundsen and Ellsworth headed for Svalbard while the crew flew the airship north. On 10 April the airship left on its long voyage to the northernmost tip of Europe and beyond.

They flew across the Mediterranean and reached the French coast by 6 pm, and at 10 pm they were at Bordeaux. They continued to fly on through the night, using only two of the three engines, and averaging 50 mph. At 7 am *Norge* left the French coast near Caen and crossed the English Channel. At 3 pm they were over Pulham, where they had to fly around for some time because of atmospheric conditions. At 5 pm they landed and were housed in Pulham's hangar next to the gigantic bulk of R-33.

At 11 pm on 13 April *Norge* set off on the flight to Oslo, where she was moored to the airship mast at 3 pm the following day. They took off again late in the evening, in a hurry because of cyclonic conditions approaching from England, and flew south of Stockholm and Helsinki to Leningrad. There was no airship hangar in Norway, and it had been arranged for them to use the one at Gatchina, where they could wait in the northernmost airship hangar on continental Europe, until weather conditions were favourable to head further north. The interest in the airship from the Russians was immense. On the first Sunday they spent in Russia about 10,000 people filed through the airship hangar to see *Norge*.

They spent three weeks at Gatchina and then began the voyage north to Svalbard on 5 May. By 5.30 am on 6 May *Norge* was moored at the mast at Vadsø, the most northern point in Norway. After six hours stay for refuelling the airship continued its journey north, arriving at the South Cape of Svalbard at 2 am on 7 May. Five hours later they were at King's Bay, despite the failure of one of the engines, which was repaired in flight.

A canvas-sided airship hangar had been built to house *Norge*, as well as a mooring mast. This had been a titanic task, begun the previous autumn, and completed through the Arctic winter working entirely by artificial light. While heading for this they could clearly see two ships in the bay, *Heimdal*, Amundsen's own depot ship, and *Chantier*, the ship that had brought Commander Byrd's expedition to Svalbard.

The Americans had arrived on 25 April, and with *Heimdal* occupying the only wharf had been forced to anchor offshore. Byrd had been forced to bring one of his Fokker Monoplanes, The *Josephine Ford*, ashore on a makeshift pontoon, made by lashing four boats together. As soon as *Norge*, arrived on 7 May, Byrd was quick to ask Nobile when he would be heading for the Pole, and was told it would be in about three days. The Americans made frantic last-minute preparations, and at 1.30 am on 9 May the Norwegians were awoken by the sound of aero-engines. They rushed outside in time to see the *Josephine Ford* roaring off on her flight to the North Pole.

All that day the Norwegians were busy making their final preparations, all the time wondering what was happening to Byrd and his crew. At 5 pm an Italian mechanic rushed into the dining hall to say he could hear approaching engines. Everyone rushed outside and there was the Fokker winging in from the north, safe and sound, on their return from the first ever flight to the North Pole.

On 9 May Amundsen was ready to go on his second attempt to reach the North Pole by air. This time, drawing on the experience of being stranded on the ice pack with no communications, he was well equipped with radio. *Norge* was equipped with a long wave transmitter and receiver powered by a propeller-driven generator, which had a range of 2000 miles in the interference-free air of the Arctic. On the flight to Pulham the airship had established two-way communications with London while still off the south coast of France. *Norge* was also equipped with powerful direction-finding equipment, which included two aerial loops, wound around the complete outer envelope.

On 11 May *Norge* set off on her voyage across the top of the world, with sixteen men on board. Amundsen and Ellsworth were the joint leaders of the aerial expedition, but Nobile was the captain of the airship. Second in command was Riiser-Larsen, and First Lieutenant Emil Horgen of the Norwegian Navy was assigned to the side rudder, with the main rudder in the care of a chief gunner of the Norwegian Navy, Oscar Wisting. Captain Birger Gottwaldt was the radio expert with Frithjof Storm-Johnsen the radio telegraphist. Fredrik Ramm was a journalist who filed regular reports by radio, and Finn Malmgren was their meteorologist. Oskar Omdahl and five Italiam mechanics made up the rest of the crew.

At 9.55 am the airship was let go, and set course for the north. Byrd took off just afterwards and accompanied the airship for about an hour. The fifteen-hour flight to the Pole was uneventful, only the monotony of the jagged ice field lay below them, with two glimpses of polar bears the only cause for excitement. It has to be remembered that at the time it was not known whether the Arctic consisted entirely of sea, or contained land masses or islands of whatever size.

At 1.25 pm Greenwich Mean Time they circled the Pole and dropped the Norwegian, Italian and American flags. They then set course for Alaska, across a part of the globe that had never been seen by human eyes. At 8.30 am they ran into a thick belt of fog that did not clear until 6 pm. The fog caused ice to form on all the metal parts of the airship, and when it broke off it often damaged the envelope after being hurled into it by the propellers. Constant repairs had to be made.

At 6.45 am on 13 May the coast of Alaska was sighted, twenty-nine hours after leaving the Pole. Soon they were over Wainwright, which Amundsen recognised having been there in 1922–3. They then ran into a gale and had to battle against it over the Bering Strait. Finally, *Norge* reached the village of Teller, 90 miles from Nome, after seventy hours in the air. A member of the crew parachuted to the ground to supervise the landing, and anchor and landing ropes were dropped. The landing was successfully accomplished and the airship was deflated. The first flight across the North Pole had been accomplished, and the use of a semi-rigid airship had been justified.

Amundsen had become the first man to reach both Poles, and decided that his career in exploration was over. He retired to a quiet life, his finances having been restored by the success of *Norge*.

After the expedition Umberto Nobile began planning another airship flight across the Arctic, but this time with more scientific aims in mind. He planned several flights over the ice pack, and invented a device for lowering men onto the surface from a hovering airship, so that scientific measurements could be made. Mussolini approved this plan in October 1927, and Nobile was given permission to acquire the sister airship of *Norge*, *Italia*. The Italian Air Ministry supplied the crew and the Italian Geographical Society planned the scientific programme. The whole expedition, which included a steamship as a floating base, which was renamed *City of Milan*, was financed by that city.

Three scientists accompanied Nobile, led by Finn Malmgren, who had been on *Norge*. Three flights were made in all from King's Bay, Svalbard, the first being on 11 May 1928, with thirteen men on board. The weather deteriorated and *Italia* turned back to the north coast of the island. Four days later Nobile set off once more, this time in an easterly direction, past the north coast of Franz Josef Land and Severnaya Zemlya. Banks of low-lying cloud forced Nobile to return to Svalbard once more.

The last flight of *Italia* began at 4.51 am on 23 May 1928. The airship flew north against the wind on a course towards Cape Bridgman in north-east Greenland. They soon crossed the edge of the ice pack, and flew on until Greenland was sighted at 2.45 pm. The wind had reduced the speed of *Italia* to only 37 mph.

At 5.29 pm near Cape Bridgman Nobile set course for the North Pole. With a following wind, and sunny weather *Italia* made good time and the North Pole was reached at 2.20 am, on 24 May. Nobile and the six others in the crew, who had also been on *Norge*, became the first people to fly over

13. *Italia* leaving King's Bay, Svalbard, on 23 May 1928 for the North Pole. The airship failed to make the return journey, crashing on the ice.

the North Pole for a second time. Nobile had intended to use his invention to lower some people onto the ice to make scientific observations, but the wind speed was too great, so they contented themselves with dropping the Pope's Cross and the Italian flag from a height of 500 feet.

They turned south running on longitudinal 25 degrees east at a height of 3000 feet. Cloud was encountered until 10 pm, and then they descended to 700 feet, where they were able to work out their ground speed, which was only 26 mph. They had been running on only two of the three engines for the whole of the flight, but now the third was started. Even with all three engines running the ground speed at 3.25 am was still only 43 mph.

They were running in gale force winds with thick banks of fog, interspersed with snow storms. The crew were becoming anxious, desperate for landfall, and then at 9.25 am the elevator jammed, probably caused by ice. The airship dived, and to prevent it striking the ice Nobile stopped all engines. *Italia* slowly rose to 3000 feet while repairs to the elevator were being made. At 9.55 am repairs were adjudged complete and two engines were started. The airship cautiously descended to 1000 feet.

At 10.30 am, when *Italia* was 45 miles north-east of Ross Island and 180 miles from King's Bay, it developed a strong list to the stern. The airship had been light and therefore they were holding the nose down to maintain level flight. Nobile had just dropped a glass ball of red liquid from a starboard porthole. He was timing its fall to the ice, to check their exact height, when he heard Cecioni, one of the Italian crewmen, exclaiming that they were heavy. This was probably because of the loss of gas caused by the ice being flung into the envelope by the propellers.

When Nobile ducked his head back inside the gondola he found they were down about 8 degrees by the tail, and descending quickly. He quickly ordered the two engines that were running to be brought to full power, and to start the other engine. He hoped to increase their forward speed and therefore the dynamic lift of the airship, to arrest their descent. He stared at the variometer, but it showed they were still descending, possibly even more quickly. With the ice pack getting uncomfortably near he ordered the engines to be stopped, to lessen the possibility of fire, and ordered the ballast chain dropped.

There was remarkable calm in the gondola, as the crew obeyed orders silently. The port engine was still running, and Nobile shouted from a porthole to the mechanic, Caratti, to shut it down. As he did so he looked down, to the stern, and saw the rear gondola was only a few metres above the ice. He ducked back inside again and grabbed the wheel, hoping to steer *Italia* onto the ice to lessen the impact. With a resounding crash the rear gondola hit the ice pack, killing the mechanic there. The control car then hit, and as it was dragged across the ice ridges it was torn away from the keel. The lightened airship immediately rose back into the air, with one wall of the control car still attached. There were six men still on board, as the unpowered airship drifted up, and with the wind back towards the Pole.

The gondola had broken open under the impact and the other nine men were spilled on the ice together with provisions and equipment. When the men had recovered from the shock of being suddenly deposited on the

Arctic ice pack as *Italia* floated away into the sky, they took stock of their position. Luckily, the emergency radio had fallen with them, and appeared to be undamaged. They began sending distress signals to *City of Milan* but the ship did not appear to be listening.

They continued to send messages every hour as they made themselves secure in the remains of the gondola. They were on a drifting ice floe, which travelled 28 miles south-east over the next two days. On 28 May Charles XII Land came into view and Malmgren and two others, Mariano and Zappi, were detailed to walk across the ice in the hope of finding help. Those remaining continued to send SOS messages and finally, on 6 June, an operator in Archangel replied.

A huge relief operation was set in motion, co-ordinated by the Norwegian Government, and Roald Amundsen was naturally asked to take a leading part. Amundsen and Nobile had fallen out, however, and the Norwegian had said things about his Italian colleague that caused Mussolini to specifically request that he should not be in any way involved with the search and rescue attempt. Amundsen returned home, but was desperate to help, and not to be seen to be standing idly by while his former companion was lost on the ice. Vividly recalling his own three-week ordeal on the Arctic ice pack, he was desperate to help.

By the intervention of a Norwegian business man in Paris, he secured the use of a French Latham 47 flying boat from the Aviation Maritime, together with its crew of Captaine de Corvette Rene Guildad; co-pilot, Lieutenant Cavelier de Cuverville; a radio officer, Emile Valette; and mechanic, Gilbert Brazy. The Latham 47 was a biplane flying boat with two Renault 12 JB engines in a tandem arrangement. The search for *Italia* had become an international event, and national prestige was at stake, which is why the French were so willing to send one of their most modern flying boats, even

14. Lundberg's aircraft after crashing on the ice, during his second landing at the crash-site, adding himself to the five men stranded on the ice.

15. The Latham 47 flying boat, borrowed by Roald Amundsen to search for *Italia*, and in which he went missing.

though twenty other aircraft were already involved.

The *Latham* left Caudebec on Saturday 16 June and arrived at Bergen, Norway, that same evening. After a 24 hour rest they flew on to Tromsø. Here, they were joined by Amundsen and his fellow pilot Lief Dietrichson. The aircraft was carefully prepared at Tromsø. Ten hours later, at 4 pm on Monday 18 June it took off on its last flight. Shortly afterwards a fisherman saw the aircraft flying into a fog bank, while apparently trying to climb above it. The last heard of Amundsen and the *Latham* was a radio message received three hours later. The flying boat was never seen again, but ten weeks later, on 13 October, one of the aircraft's petrol tanks and a float were picked up off the north-west coast of Norway, followed by more wreckage a few days later.

The tank and the float had been unscrewed from the aircraft's structure. It appeared that the *Latham* had been forced down somewhere in a disabled state, and that the crew had attempted to save themselves by creating a boat from the parts. A search was not initiated for the *Latham* for some time after its departure from Tromsø because many suspected that Amundsen might well have changed direction after take-off to make directly for Nobile's position, which would explain his non-arrival at King's Bay.

On 15 June the ice-breaker *Krassin* had sailed from Leningrad to trawl the west coast of Svalbard. Another ship the *Malyguin* searched the east coast. Riiser-Larsen searched in a Norwegian seaplane and three Swedish aircraft and an Italian seaplane also joined in the search. On 20 June the men on the ice floe were discovered by the Italian aircraft and food for twenty days was dropped to them.

16. The Russian ice-breaker *Krassin*, having just arrived at the crash-site.

A Swedish pilot named Lundberg flew out to land on the ice floe with orders to bring back Nobile himself. Despite Nobile's protestations that he should be the last man saved, he relented and was flown back to Svalbard. When Lundberg flew back to save more of the men his aircraft was wrecked while landing, returning to six the number of men stranded on the ice.

Meanwhile *Krassin* was cutting a path through the ice to the men. At one point, on 6 July, a Junkers monoplane was lowered from the ship onto the ice and began an air search. The Russian pilot spotted the Italians Mariano and Zappi near to King Charles XII Land and was able to land and rescue them. *Krassin* smashed its way through the ice to the remainder of the men and they were taken on board after an ordeal on the ice that had lasted thirty-two days.

No sign of *Italia* or the six men on board was ever found. Roald Amundsen had forced landed on the Arctic ice pack and he and his men had saved themselves by their own efforts, but he had perished trying to save others who were in the same predicament. Nevertheless, a legend built up among some of his countrymen that the 'White Eagle' of Norwegian polar exploration was out on the ice somewhere waiting rescue, and would one day return from the frozen wastes, as he always had before.

CHAPTER 6

Down in the Atlantic

Captain Frank Courtney was one of the most famous British pilots in the years following the First World War, the popular press dubbing him 'The Man with the Magic Hands'. In 1928 he made an attempt to become the first man to fly the Atlantic from east to west over the Azores route in a Dornier Wal flying boat. Both he and the aircraft succeeded in reaching America, but not together! Because of an engine fire, he and his crew parted company with the Dornier in mid-ocean, and the crew and aircraft completed the journey quite separately.

Frank Courtney looked like a bank clerk, tall and slim with pince-nez glasses, and in 1913 that is just what he was, in a Paris bank. Smitten by the thought of flying he wrote to Claude Grahame-White at his fledgling aircraft company at Hendon, and was able to talk his way into an unpaid apprenticeship.

With the help of a loan from the family solicitor, he was also able to pay for flying lessons at the Grahame-White School. One of his fellow pupils through the summer of 1914 was JD North, the chief engineer of the company. Courtney was able to obtain his certificate (No. 874) three weeks after the War started; JD North never did.

Courtney had tried to join the Royal Flying Corps the day war broke out, but was rejected because of his glasses, and returned to Hendon. As soon as the need for experienced men became apparent, he was encouraged to join the RFC as an Air Mechanic Second Class (2nd AM), and was posted to Farnborough. When it was discovered that he had a pilot's certificate (and by claiming double the three hours flying time he had accumulated), he was put on the roster of standby pilots, for when there was a shortage. Then, by volunteering to take the most inhospitable shifts, at weekends, he was made flight instructor. He was now given flying pay and was allowed to wear wings, the only 2nd AM pilot in the RFC!

A failed attempt to loop a greatly disliked Martinsyde S1 Scout, resulted in uncontrolled gyrations all over the sky, because of the effect of the rotary engine. Several further attempts had the same result, but his colleagues and superiors who had watched this performance came to the quite erroneous conclusion that he was an expert aerobatic pilot. This resulted in him being posted on a monoplane course – monoplanes being seen as tricky to fly.

Shortly afterwards he was promoted to corporal, and transferred to France, ferrying an Avro 504 in the process. As there were no corporal pilots on active service he was promoted to sergeant right away; he flew Morane Parasol monoplanes with No. 3 Squadron. After surviving 'The Fokker Scourge' and becoming an experienced battle-tested pilot, Courtney was shot down and wounded. Following his period of recuperation he was promoted to second lieutenant and posted to Farnborough as a military test pilot.

In September 1916 he returned to France to No. 20 Squadron, flying FE2ds. He later transferred to No. 45 Squadron, and then No. 70 Squadron on Sopwith 1¹/₂ Strutters. Back in No. 45 Squadron as a flight commander, he managed to survive 'Bloody April' 1917, and was then transferred back to England to take up a Special Instructor's post at London Colney. Subsequently, he was transferred back to military test flying. During this period he had his first contact with Boulton & Paul at Norwich, being involved with a programme to fit 150 hp Gnome Monosoupape engines to Sopwith Camels destined for the American forces. He also test flew the first Boulton & Paul design, the P3 Bobolink fighter.

After the War, Courtney became a freelance test pilot and Boulton & Paul, where JD North was now chief engineer, became one of his best customers. He test flew their P.7 Bourges twin-engined fighter-bomber, and achieved lasting fame by looping it, and demonstrating its aerobatic potential at Hendon and elsewhere. He flew many prototypes for numerous companies including Airco, Martinsyde, Armstrong Whitworth, Hawker Aircraft, and Koolhoven in Holland as well as Boulton & Paul. He also operated as a reserve pilot for some of the fledgling airlines of the day, and was a familiar competitor at many of the air races in the immediate post-war years.

In 1923 alone he made the first flights of the Hawker Duiker army co-operation monoplane; the Armstrong Whitworth Awana transport; Armstrong Whitworth Wolf corps-reconnaissance biplane; the Armstrong Whitworth metal-Siskin fighter; the Handasyde Monoplane; the Fokker FK31 monoplane fighter; and the Boulton & Paul Bugle bomber; as well as many other testing assignments. He flew numerous airline sectors, mostly to the Continent, to Paris, Amsterdam and Berlin; flew the Siskin on demonstration tours of Spain and Sweden; and still had time to win the King's Cup flying the Siskin II, G-EBEU, at an average speed of 149 mph!

In 1927 Courtney attempted an East–West crossing of the Atlantic, trying to attract the interest of major shipping companies in the use of flying boats for high-speed mail and parcel carriage.

He had already been involved in one attempt at a transatlantic crossing, but in the opposite direction. After the War many of the major aircraft manufacturers had turned their attention to the pre-war *Daily Mail* prize of £10,000, offered for the first non-stop flight across the Atlantic, which had been held in abeyance during the War years. One of those interested in winning both the money and the prestige was Boulton & Paul Ltd of Norwich.

The company set about converting its P7 Bourges bomber into an airliner suitable for making the first West–East crossing. The revised aircraft was designated the P8 Atlantic and construction of it was well underway in the

17. Captain Frank Courtney (second left) about to test-fly the Boulton & Paul Bolton at Mousehold Aerodrome, Norwich, in 1922. The chief engineer of Boulton & Paul, JD North is hatless with his hands on his hips.

first months of 1919, the company being aware that rival manufacturers like Sopwith, Martinsyde, Vickers, Handley Page and Short Bros were also preparing aircraft.

The volume of the P7 fuselage was increased by building up a fairing on the upper surface until it was flush with the upper wing, giving the fuselage an overall depth of 6 feet 6 inches. The central portion of this was filled with fuel tanks for the Atlantic flight, with a cabin for a navigator and second pilot at the forward end. The pilot was given a fully enclosed canopy, a very advanced feature of the day, and the power was provided by two 450 hp Napier Lion engines mounted on the lower wings. These gave sufficient power to enable the aircraft to maintain height after an engine failure (or half engine power) after two hours of fuel had been used up, a safety feature with which the other contenders were not blessed.

Frank Courtney was booked to make the first flight of the P8 Atlantic, but he was not to make the Atlantic flight itself. Major K Savory was to be the first pilot for that, Captain AL Howarth the second pilot, and Captain JH Woolner the Navigator. With the Sopwith and Martinsyde contenders for the *Daily Mail* prize already in Newfoundland, time was in short supply, and when the P8 Atlantic was ready for its first flight, in April 1919, things were rushed.

A number of dignitaries had come down from London to view the first flight, and they were anxious to catch a train back as preparations for the

18. The Boulton & Paul P8 Atlantic just before its first flight at Mousehold, in 1919.

19. The Boulton & Paul Atlantic after its first flight take-off crash.

flight went ahead. Courtney and the aircraft's mechanic, Cecil Browne, who would also be on the flight, were urged to get a move on. Yielding to the pressure, Courtney ran up the two engines individually but neglected to run them up together. As the aircraft roared into the air for the first time, at Norwich's Mousehold Airport, a fuel-flow problem, which would have been revealed by running the engines up together, caused one of the Lions to suddenly cut, and the Atlantic crashed. Both Courtney and Browne emerged unscathed from the broken nose of the aircraft, relieved, but much wiser men. It is not recorded whether the dignitaries did in fact manage to catch their train.

Four aircraft actually attempted the Atlantic flight, Harry Hawker ditching his Sopwith Atlantic halfway across; the Martinsyde Raymor crashing on take-off from Newfoundland; and the Short Shamrock ditching 12 miles out from Holyhead on the way to start an East–West attempt from the Curragh. It only remained for the Vickers Vimy of Alcock and Brown to carve their names in the annals of aviation history by making the first successful non-stop crossing.

The aircraft Courtney chose for his East–West crossing was the twin-engined Dornier Wal flying boat, fitted with Napier Lion engines. The Wal was a monoplane, more normally fitted with 300 hp Hispano-Suiza or 360 hp Rolls-Royce Eagle engines, carried in tandem in a nacelle above the 103.2 feet span wing, which itself was supported on struts well above the fuselage. Dispensing with wing-tip floats the Wal was fitted with Dornier's well-known sponsons, which projected from the fuselage sides, and

20. Courtney flying his first Wal, G-EBQO, named *Whale*, the aircraft that the Amundsen/Ellsworth Expedition had force-landed on the ice. It was reconditioned by the Dornier company before being sold to Courtney.

bestowed excellent sea-keeping qualities on the design.

Before Courtney's first attempt the Dornier Wal had already been used in four transatlantic attempts. The first was in April 1924, when an Italian team of Lieutenants Antonio Locatelli, V Crossio, C Marescalchi and Rissili had set out in an Italian-built Wal from Pisa in an attempt to make the first East–West crossing by a heavier-than-air aircraft. They flew via Marseilles, Lausanne, Strasbourg, Rotterdam, Brough and Reykjavik in Iceland where they caught up with the American team of Douglas World Cruisers, which was in the process of making the first round-the-world flight, in easy stages.

They agreed to fly in company with the Americans to Greenland, but after take-off it soon became clear that the Dornier was too fast to stay with the slow Douglas seaplanes, and Locatelli sped on. He flew into very bad weather and decided to land on the sea, about 200 miles east of Cape Farewell, to wait it out.

Force-landing a flying boat on the open ocean, even one as sturdy as the Dornier Wal, is always a risky business, and Locatelli and his crew were soon aware that they had made a mistake. The seas began to pound his aircraft to pieces, and it was soon unable to take off. They drifted helplessly, hoping for rescue, and once they were overdue a search was initiated. Two American cruisers, *Richmond* and *Raleigh*, searched 12,000 square miles of ocean, and on the third day a light was spotted by *Richmond* from a distance of about 10 miles. The four men were taken on board the warship, but the flying boat could not be salvaged. It was set on fire, sinking shortly afterwards.

In 1926 another Wal was prepared to fly the Atlantic, also east to west. The pilot was Ramon Franco, whose brother General Francisco Franco would later achieve much greater fame. His crew were Captain Julio Ruiz de Alda and Pablo Rada. On 22 January they took off from Huelva, near to where Columbus had departed and headed for the Canaries. They were delayed at Las Palmas until 26 January when they took off for the Cape Verde Islands. From there they flew to the island of Fernando de Noronha, 540 km from the Brazilian coast. They landed by a ship 20 miles short and taxied the rest of the way. On 31 January they completed the first crossing of the South Atlantic by aviators using the same aircraft all the way.

In 1927 there were to be two more attempted crossings in Dornier Wals before Frank Courtney's. A Uruguyan team of Larre Borges and Captain Ibara in a Wal with two 500 hp Farman engines left Pisa on 20 February 1927, on the first stage of a round-the-world attempt. They flew via Alicante and Casablanca, but on the way to Agadir, on the Morrocan coast, a broken oil pipe caused them to attempt a forced landing. They came down in a trough of the waves, were hit broadside on and the Wal was carried onto the beach where it was smashed.

The following month the Portuguese crew of Sarmento Beires, Jorge de Castilho, Manuel Gouveia and Dovalle Portugal, left Lisbon on 3 March, in a Wal powered by two 450 hp Lorraine-Dietrich engines. They flew via Casablanca, Villa Cisneros and Portuguese Guinea, where they had difficulty getting off the water with a full load. They finally got away on 11 March, and crossed to Brazil with a stop at Fernando de Noronha.

Frank Courtney's 1927 attempt was organised with undue haste, which was soon to show. After flying for nearly 1000 miles from Plymouth towards the Azores, Courtney was forced to turn back to Lisbon, because of failing equipment. He had to abandon the attempt until the following year. There had now been five attempted Atlantic crossings using Dornier Wals, two had succeeded and three had failed, two after disastrous forced landings. The adverse odds did not deter Frank Courtney, however.

His second attempt in 1928 was a better organised affair, bankrolled by a wealthy Canadian named Elwood Hosmer, who insisted on going along on the flight, nominally serving as steward. A brand new Dornier Wal was purchased from the factory, which had been established at Pisa in Italy to bypass restrictions on German aircraft production. A Canadian registration was obtained, G-CAJI. The Napier company again loaned him two Lion engines, and the Marconi Company provided the radio equipment.

There were to be two other crew members, Hugh Gilmour, an experienced marine radio operator from Marconi, and a flight mechanic named Fred Pierce. The flight would be directly from Pisa to Lisbon, where Gilmour would join, and then via the Azores to Newfoundland.

A preliminary flight test revealed a major problem, the signals from the radio direction finder (DF) could not be heard above the sound of the engine ignition noise. After a great deal of head scratching, a simple but ridiculous solution was adopted. Courtney would throttle back the engines to idle, and glide the flying boat while the radio operator took his bearing, it being found possible to do this against the small amount of interference remaining.

With this problem solved they were ready to go, and left Pisa in mid-June for the thirteen-hour flight to Lisbon. Here they waited for Gilmour who, when he finally arrived, announced that he had never been in an aircraft

21. Courtney's second Dornier Wal, G-CAJI, at Pisa, ready to start its flight to America, via Lisbon. Courtney is standing in the cockpit.

before! Flying the Atlantic on your first flight might not be unusual these days, but in 1928 it was extraordinary. However, Gilmour was only concerned with the quality of the radio equipment, and did not seem at all concerned that he might be one of the first crew to fly the Atlantic on the Azores route, east to west. Nevertheless, he was given a few practice flights to familiarise himself with the use of the equipment in the air, and in particular the eccentric direction-finding procedure.

Finally, they left Lisbon early on 28 June and set course for the Azores, cruising at 10,000 feet. Everything went well, even the direction-finding, with regular bearings being taken on the station at São Miguel island. After a flight of thirteen hours they landed in Horta harbour, hoping to continue to Newfoundland after refuelling. Unfortunately, two problems arose, firstly two wires in the DF loop had come adrift, and the constant-speed drive of the air-driven transmitting generator had broken. Obtaining a replacement by ship would take weeks, so they set about making one with the primitive facilities that were available. After three weeks of trial and error they finally made one that did not fail, and were able to continue their journey.

They left Horta early in the morning against a moderate headwind, but beyond the islands of Flores and Corvo the wind strengthened. Gilmour managed to raise a ship about 400 miles ahead of them, which was buffeting through a 35 mph westerly gale with the barometer falling rapidly. With the elements against him Courtney turned back, and sped back to Horta in half the time, landing wearily after a twelve-hour flight.

He decided in the light of that experience that an evening take-off would be preferable, so that they would definitely arrive in Newfoundland in daylight. On 1 August at 5 pm they took off again on what was to be G-CAJI's last flight. At 6.30 pm they passed Flores and Corvo once more, with the sun setting behind ominously black clouds on the horizon ahead.

Courtney had never flown the Dornier at night or in a thunderstorm, but he was confident of his abilities. He told his crew to fix down everything they could, fasten their seat belts and hold on tight. He flew into the storm at 1500 feet, low enough, he hoped, to avoid the worst of the updrafts, but far enough above the stormy waters to give him a margin of error.

The storm was a violent one, with torrential rain and occasional hail battering the aircraft. There was almost continuous lightning, and the altimeter showed several hundred feet of height changes. Concentrating on the Reid turn indicator to try and keep the Dornier level, against the abrupt changes of attitude, Courtney found the big flying boat as easy to fly in such conditions as he might have hoped. He settled down for a long battle against the elements, which in fact went on for two hours.

They then emerged from the storm, beneath an overcast sky. Courtney told Gilmour to wind out his aerial and to start searching for Newfoundland stations. It was just before midnight, and they were eight hours into the flight, just over half the distance to their destination. With no warning, disaster struck.

Suddenly, one of the Lions began backfiring, and then there was an orange glow on the windscreen. Pierce shouted that the rear engine was on fire. Courtney looked back and all he could see was the terrifying sight of a flood of burning fuel pouring from the rear engine, and a long trail of black smoke and fiery sparks. Courtney cut the switches and put the nose down. He headed for the safety of the surface of the sea, in a dive as steep as he dared, hoping he could pull out once he could see its surface.

Pierce remembered that the only cut-off for the gravity tank was up in the nacelle, and with the propellers still turning, fuel was still being pumped into the flames. He struggled out onto the aircraft's hull, and reached up into the small access hole between the two engines. He was still desperately turning off the fuel cock, buffeted by the slipstream, when they hit the water. Gilmour had rapidly wound the aerial back in and sat philosophically waiting the worst. Hosmer had a small cabin right beneath the blazing engine. He stayed there, out of the way, as long as he could, but the raging heat had soon driven him forward.

Courtney had seen the surface when they were at about 200 feet, and skimmed the breakers, which were glowing red from the flames of the burning aircraft swooping over them. With hard left rudder he set the flying boat down, expecting a fierce crunch, but the hull slid quietly onto the water. Before he could breathe a sigh of relief they ran right into a huge wave, which brought them to a halt with a shattering crash.

There was no time to congratulate themselves for their safe arrival on the sea. The flames that had been trailing aft were now playing around the engine nacelle, consuming odd pools of fuel and threatening to explode the ten main fuel tanks below. Pierce squirted their little 2-pound fire extinguisher into the flames, with no visible effect. Then all they could do was cling to the outside of the hull, drenched in spray, waiting for the

explosion. They felt utterly helpless, but after ten minutes or so the flames died down. Pierce's incredibly courageous act in turning off the fuel cocks had probably saved them.

Courtney returned to the controls, and began sailing the flying boat into the wind using the rudder and ailerons, while Pierce and Gilmour launched their sea-anchor. They rode out the rest of the night, the sea-anchor keeping them into the wind, and the steady sea-keeping qualities of the

22. **The burnt-out Napier Lion engine of the Wal, photographed in mid-Atlantic, while the crew were awaiting rescue.**

Dornier's sponsors keeping them upright.

At dawn they decided to try and take-off using the forward engine. Courtney started the remaining Lion and opened the throttle to try a test run. If everything went well, they would then jettison some fuel and take-off. No sooner had the aircraft began moving than Pierce shouted in alarm. The damaged engine was rocking so badly it was threatening to fall from its damaged mountings and through the hull. Courtney quickly switched off the engine, and they resumed floating, Gilmour sending out distress signals.

Their first SOS had been picked up by the liner *Cedric*, which organised communications with other shipping, and the Shell tanker *Achatina* and other ships headed for them. At 4 pm the German liner *Columbus* reached the position they had broadcast, but the wind and Gulf Stream had by then carried them miles away. Worst still, their small battery was by now nearly dead, so that they could no longer send signals. All they could do was sit tight and hope one of the ships would find them.

It was growing dusk when the liner SS *Minnewaska* sailed into view, and they were taken on board with their small bag of mail. There was no means of salvaging the Dornier, so that was left to drift in mid-Atlantic. Four days later they arrived in New York, and were surprised to be greeted with a hero's welcome.

Even G-CAJI made it across the ocean. The Italian freighter *Valprato* came across it and took it on board. Two days later it docked in Montreal. Unfortunately, the aircraft's structure had been so damaged when the

23. The SS *Minnewaska* arriving to rescue Courtney and the Wal's crew.

24. The *Minnewaska's* lifeboat approaching the Wal, which had been drifting for 19 hours.

freighter's crew had lifted it, that it was a write-off. At least Napier got their engines back, one rather damaged. They discovered that the fire had been caused by a backfire igniting fuel leaking from a copper fuel line crystalised through vibration.

Elwood Hosmer, who had bought the aircraft, and very nearly lost his life, proclaimed that he had never had so much fun! Frank Courtney, his services soon no longer required as a freelance test pilot because companies such as Armstrong Whitworth and Boulton & Paul took on full-time test pilots, moved to the United States. He continued a distinguished career there, most notably concerned with the airline use of flying boats, and as a World War Two ferry pilot.

He was to fly the Atlantic many times, in both directions, and later went on to work for Convair. He finally retired to La Jolla, California, when he was 65 years old, after 43 years in the aircraft business. Dornier Wal flying boats were also to make many more Atlantic crossings, pioneering Lufthansa, services which featured mid-Atlantic refuelling points and even catapult launches from ships.

CHAPTER 7

Down in the Outback

Australia is a large country, or a small continent, depending on your point of view. What is not in dispute is that the interior includes huge tracts of uninhabited and inhospitable countryside. The outback is a dangerous place in which to make a forced landing, but parts of it, in the Northern Territory, include even greater hazards than the unforgiving climate – some of the biggest crocodiles in the world.

Sir Charles Kingsford-Smith is probably the most famous aviator Australia has ever produced, forever associated with the Fokker Monoplane *Southern Cross* and the long-distance flying exploits he undertook in it, as well as other aircraft. He actually began his flying career in the First World War, joining the Royal Flying Corps on his eighteenth birthday, and later wounded flying against the Turks.

25. Charles Kingsford-Smith in front of the *Southern Cross*.

After the War he bought four DH6s and operated them in the London area for a short while. He had ambitions to make a name for himself as an aviator, and in particular by winning the £10,000 prize for being the first Australian to fly from England to Australia. The Australian Prime Minister had expressly forbidden him from being an entry in that contest because of his youth, and the prize was duly won by Captain Ross Smith and Lieutenant Keith Smith, brothers, and pilots in the Royal Australian Air Force, with their mechanics WH Shiers and JM Bennett.

He moved to California for a short while, taking whatever flying jobs he could find, but then moved back to his native land where he went to work for Western Australia Airways, who had obtained an airmail contract and purchased six Bristol Tourers to operate it. In one of these, on 7 February 1922, Kingsford-Smith is credited with flying the first 'flying doctor' service in the country when he flew a child with diptheria from way out in the outback to hospital.

From 1924 onwards the Bristol Tourers were gradually replaced by DH50s. Kingsford-Smith and his friend Keith Anderson, purchased two Bristol Tourers, G-AUDJ and G-AUDK, and started Interstate Flying Services. In January 1927 they flew one from Perth to Sydney in an unsuccessful bid to break the Trans-Australia record. At this time Charles Ulm was appointed as Interstate's manager.

In June 1927, to prove himself as a long-distance aviator, Kingsford-Smith flew G-AUDK, in company with Charles Ulm, around the coastline of Australia, 7500 miles in 10 days 5 hours. This flight was repeated with Anderson and Bob Hitchcock crewing the Tourer on charter to the George A Bond & Co. Hosiery company, with Charles Vivian representing the company – a sales tour that circled the continent in a more leisurely manner.

Armed with the prestige accrued after these flights Kingsford-Smith, Ulm, and Anderson devised a plan to become the first to fly the Pacific, and the Prime Minister of Australia promised financial support.

They set off for America but it was to be nine months before their return. The money promised by the Government was not enough to buy a capable aircraft, even though they obtained the agreement of George Hubert Wilkins (later knighted), a famous explorer, then living in America, to sell them his Fokker Monoplane. The aircraft was something of an amalgamation of two aircraft owned by Wilkins. The first was a Fokker F.VIIB/3m, a three-engined Fokker assembled by the Atlantic Aircraft Corporation at Teterborough, New Jersey, from parts made in Holland. It had an extra large 728 square feet wing of 71 feet 2 inches span. The second was a single-engined Fokker F.VII, built in Holland and powered by a 420 hp Liberty engine, and had a 63 feet 4 inches wingspan.

Both aircraft were shipped to Alaska in 1926 for use in Wilkins' Arctic exploration. The single-engined aircraft was named *Alaska* and the larger aircraft was named *Detroiter* after the two areas of the United States from which most of the sponsorship for the expedition had been drawn. It was while in Alaska that the two aircraft almost became involved in the search for Roald Amundsen, when he force-landed on the Arctic ice pack.

The larger Fokker crashed in Alaska, damaging the fuselage. In the following year Wilkins returned to Alaska, with two Stinson SB-1 biplanes, and a hybrid of the two Fokkers which he hoped to use for long distance surveys. He combined the wing of the three-engined F.VIIB/3m and the fuselage of the F.VII. The resulting aircraft was not entirely satisfactory, and was not used operationally.

The surviving parts were taken to Boeing Aircraft at Seattle. Boeing returned the three-engined aircraft to its original form, but a new fin and rudder of larger area was added. It was this aircraft that was offered to Kingsford-Smith. The remains of Wilkins' single-engined F.VII, just the fuselage and tail surfaces, eventually found their way to the Historical Society of Bismarck, North Dakota.

Eventually, Kingsford-Smith obtained the necessary backing to buy the Fokker for £3000 from an ex-patriate businessman, named Myer. He also paid for new instrumentation and three new 220 hp Wright Whirlwind engines. The aircraft was also fitted out with new fuel tankage, raising the total from 320 gallons to 1080 gallons, and giving the aircraft a still air range of 3679 miles. This work was apparently done at Douglas Aircraft, who also painted the aircraft. The fuselage was painted standard US Army Air Corps light blue, and the wings gold, with the word 'Fokker' in black on white panels.

They still did not have enough money to finance the flight, and failed in an attempt to win a large prize available to anyone breaking the world record endurance of 52 hours 22 minutes. Even with an extra forty-five 5-gallon tins in the cabin they had to land after 50 hours 4 minutes of trundling round San Francisco Bay. On switching off the engines, they only had 5 minutes fuel left.

Admitting defeat, they flew the *Southern Cross*, as they had named the aircraft (not after the southern constellation on the Australian flag, but after the town from where Kingsford-Smith was born), to California, hoping to sell the aircraft to recoup the money.

Fortunately, there they met an ex-master mariner named Captain Allan Hancock, who happened to be the President of the California Bank. He agreed to put up the money for the flight. On the morning of 31 May 1928 *Southern Cross* was ready at Oakland, California, fully fuelled, with 96 gallons in each of the four wing tanks, another 107 gallons in a tank under the pilot's seat and 807 gallons in a massive fuselage tank. Kingsford-Smith and Charles Ulm were the pilots, but Keith Anderson had returned to Australia. There he made an attempt to fly to England in one of the old Tourers, together with Bob Hitchcock, but they crashed at Pine Creek, Northern Territory. Two Americans were recruited to make up the crew of *Southern Cross* for the Pacific flight; Harry Lyon was to be the navigator and James Warner the wireless operator.

They flew the Pacific in three stages, the first being to Wheeler Field, Honolulu, and the next, the longest at 3138 miles, to Suva in Fiji. The last lap to Brisbane was the shortest at only 1700 miles, but certainly not the easiest. They flew into a massive storm, with high winds and torrential rain, so heavy it broke the windscreens and soaked the cockpit. Fighting the bucking aircraft almost totally exhausted the crew, and they were very near

26. *Southern Cross* **in flight over North America.**

the end of their tether when the coast of Queensland was finally sighted, 110 miles south of their intended track.

They became heroes overnight and decorations and financial rewards were showered on them. The two Americans, Warner and Lyon, returned to America and HA Litchfield joined the crew as navigator, and TH McWilliams as wireless operator. They made three more epic flights in quick succession, across the continent non-stop, and then across the Tasman Sea to New Zealand and back. *Southern Cross* was now registered G-AUSU, having retained its US serial 1985 for the Pacific flight.

Following these three further record-breaking triumphs, they planned a flight to England. Although they would be attempting the record, the trip had another purpose. Kingsford-Smith had founded Australian National Airways Ltd, and wished to visit European manufacturers to negotiate for the purchase of aircraft, specifically Avro 10s, which were licence-built Fokker F.VIIB/3ms.

At midday on 31 March 1929 *Southern Cross* took off from Richmond Airfield, just outside Sydney, for the first stage of the flight, the 2000 miles to Singleton. Alongside Kingsford-Smith in the cockpit was Charles Ulm, as second pilot. In the rear cabin were HA Litchfield, the navigator, and TH McWilliams, the wireless operator. Between this rear cabin and the cockpit was the huge fuselage fuel tank, and the only communication possible between them was to write messages on bits of paper and to pass them over this tank at the end of a stick.

Shortly after take-off the long-range aerial was lost. Litchfield leaned out of the window to take a sight with the drift indicator, and his arm caught a button that controlled the copper wire aerial. There was enough wire wound on the drum to make three aerials, in case one or more were broken off and

27. The pilot's cockpit of *Southern Cross.*

carried away on landing. The whole length of wire unreeled and was lost, which meant they could no longer receive, though they could still transmit.

Kingsford-Smith decided to continue the flight, because the weather reports they had received before take-off had forecast good weather. Though there was no real reason to abort the flight in the circumstances, the decision was to have tragic consequences.

Soon after they crossed the centre of the continent the weather changed dramatically and they found themselves caught in a storm that raged through the night. Sydney had been sending warnings of this storm, but they were unable to hear them. Dawn brought little relief, but visibility was still poor, and the country they were flying over was a wilderness of forested ravines. They came to a ravine, which they followed to the west, fully expecting to find Wyndham at the end of it, but all they found was a barren coastline being battered by an angry sea. Kingsford-Smith decided to fly round Cape Londonderry to fix their position and then south-west to Wyndham.

Two hours passed by and there was still no sign of the Cape. Then they flew over a group of huts, which they later discovered was Drysdale Mission. Ulm wrote out a message in pencil and dropped it to the people they could see on the ground, asking if they could point the way to Wyndham, which they expected would now be in a south-easterly direction. They were taken by surprise when the people on the ground pointed to the south-west. It seemed incredible that they could be so much off-course, even allowing for the effect of the storm. However they reasoned that they should rely on local knowledge.

Kingsford-Smith turned to the south-west and flew on through the bad weather. Still there was no sign of Wyndham, but then they flew over another group of huts. As Kingsford-Smith circled, Ulm quickly wrote out another message and dropped it to the curious spectators on the ground. This time he asked them to place a row of white sheets on the ground indicating the direction of Wyndham, and to give in large figures the distance in miles. To the surprise of the airmen the direction indicated was east and the distance given was 250 miles. They knew that one of the two groups of people was wrong, but which one?

The second set of directions seemed more definite, and Kingsford-Smith therefore set course to the east, though he knew they had little hope of getting there. About an hour later they began to run out of fuel, and Kingsford-Smith began to look for a place for a forced landing. Much of the area was covered in the sub-tropical jungle of Northern Australia, but he saw a large clearing and headed for that. When the wheels touched down they realised why there were no trees in this area; it was a swamp.

The aircraft slowed quickly in the clinging mud, and began to nose over, but luckily fell back, coming to a halt without damage,. However, when they clambered out they found the main wheels buried up to their axles. The surrounding jungle was virtually impassable, and was intersected with creeks, and the winding River Glenelg, in which there were many crocodiles. None of the crew had the slightest intention of going for help, as this would mean crossing these crocodile-infested waters. They were stranded where they were, but their one consolation was that McWilliams had been sending out a continuous stream of radio messages, reporting on their progress, though, of course, there was no way of knowing if these had been picked up. Also, during the landing the transmitter was damaged so that they could no longer send messages, which might have helped the searchers to home in on them.

There was nothing more that they could do except wait for rescue, but when they looked for the emergency rations that should have been stowed on the Fokker they could not find them. They never did discover why they were not on board, but luckily there was a small supply of baby food that they had been transporting to Wyndham. Clouds of mosquitoes assaulted them during the night, to be replaced by black masses of flies during the day.

McWilliams set to work and managed to get the radio receiver working, so they could at least hear the efforts that were being made to find them. It was a comfort to know that searches were being made by both land and water. The great white wing of the Fokker, over 71 feet in span, should have made an excellent landmark from the air, but in addition they prepared a fire, which they kept burning in the hope that searching aircraft would see the smoke.

The heat was exhausting, and they were continuously plagued by the flies and mosquitoes. By the second day they were beginning to suffer from the effects of hunger, and by the fourth day the threat of starvation was becoming very real. They had no means of catching fish, even if they were prepared to risk the crocodiles, and though they tried the snails they found they were not at all palatable. They struggled to find sufficient dry wood to keep the fire going in the damp conditions which prevailed. Litchfield took sights, which established their position as 150 miles from Wyndham, and about 15 miles from the coast. It was an area first explored by an Englishman named George Grey almost 100 years before, and it was he who had named the river after Lord Glenelg. Grey had almost died of exhaustion trying to find his way out of the wilderness.

McWilliams, by diligent efforts, had repaired the transmitter and to power it they rigged up a friction drive. They dug out one of the main wheels so that it could revolve, and one of them turned it with a spanner, while McWilliams held the generator against it. So weak were they, however, that the combined efforts of Kingsford-Smith and Ulm could only keep the heavy mainwheel turning for a few seconds – far too little for their rescuers to home in on the weak signal.

Three times, searching aircraft passed in sight of the four men but somehow did not see the great white wing of the Fokker, or the trail of smoke in the sky. Three times their hopes were raised and then almost immediately dashed. They heard all the details of the search effort on their radio, including the further drama when one of Kingsford-Smith's former colleagues, Keith Anderson, and his mechanic Bob Hitchcock, who had joined in the aerial search in their aircraft Kookaburra, were also missing.

Finally, a de Havilland DH66 Hercules airliner of West Australian Airways, which had been chartered by the Search Committee, flew over the downed Fokker. Captain Holden, the pilot, circled round as the four downed men waved and cheered. He dropped a note and some food, and flew away. Every day for five days an aircraft returned and dropped food, and the condition of the four men slowly improved.

All the time the surface of the clearing in which they had landed was

28. The attempt to turn the Fokker's mainwheel into a dynamo, with one man turning it with a spanner.

drying up, and nineteen days after their forced landing two rescue aircraft were able to land alongside the Fokker, bringing fuel and spare parts. The *Southern Cross* took off once more and completed the journey to Wyndham, it's crew safe and well, but the episode had claimed two victims. Anderson and Hitchcock had died when their aircraft crashed. They were found by an air search by the Qantas pilot Lester Brain.

A Committee of Inquiry was set up to investigate the episode, and public opinion had turned against Kingsford-Smith, formerly a great hero, for his decision to press on after they had lost the aerial. The decision had cost the lives of two men. There were even suggestions that the whole thing had been planned as some sort of publicity stunt.

The crew of the *Southern Cross* were criticised, but the worst charge that could be levelled at them was that they were guilty of an error of judgement, which was very easy to see in the bright light of hindsight. The real reason for the forced landing turned out to be the fact that the first village to which they had dropped a message had not seen it, and merely pointed to the nearest place where a landing could be made, not to Wyndham as they thought. The diversion had caused them to run out of fuel, and made a forced landing inevitable.

To highlight the difficulties, within weeks of their rescue a third aircraft went missing in the same area. The single-engined Vickers Vellore biplane, which was being ferried out to Australia by SJ Moir and HC Owen, went missing after leaving Koepang to cross the Timor Sea. Once more it was Lester Brain who found them. He searched the coastline and eventually found the wreckage of the aircraft near Cape Don. The two men had survived the crash, and were able to signal from the ground. Brain was able to arrange their rescue by boat.

With his prestige at a low ebb, and sorrowful for the death of the two men who had been trying to rescue him, both of whom were his friends, Kingsford-Smith set off once more for England in *Southern Cross*, taking with him the same three crew members. They reached Croydon in the record time of 12 days 18 hours. He took the aircraft to the Fokker Works at Amsterdam, to be overhauled, and returned to Australia to continue with the organisation of Australian National Airways. While the aircraft was being refurbished in the Fokker Works it was painted a much darker blue, and the new registration VH-ASU was applied to it. At the same time longer engine nacelles were also fitted.

When his aircraft was ready he intended to fly across the Atlantic and then continue across America and the Pacific to complete a circuit of the world at almost its greatest circumference. On 24 June 1929 *Southern Cross* was once more ready for a momentous flight. Fully-fuelled, it stood on the beach at Portmarnock, Ireland, with three crew members: Kingsford-Smith and his new navigator, the Dutchman, Evert van Dyk, and wireless operator JW Stannage. At 4.25 am they took off and headed west across the cold waters of the Atlantic. They landed at Harbour Grace, Newfoundland, after 31.5 hours in the air. They then flew across America, via New York, to Oakland Airport, completing their circumnavigation of the Earth. Some regard this as the first circumnavigation, as the American Army fliers of

1924 who are usually credited with the feat, did not cross the Equator on any point of their circumnavigation.

For his next exploit, Kingsford-Smith attempted to beat Bert Hinkler's record for an England-to-Australia flight, and for the purpose abandoned his faithful Fokker monoplane. Avro built a special long-range Avian for him, which he christened *Southern Cross Junior*. In this he took off from Heston Airfield on 9 October 1930, and arrived at Port Darwin on the afternoon of the 19th, having beaten the record, achieving the flight in fewer than ten days.

His prestige was totally restored in his native land. In 1931 he failed in an attempt to break Jim Mollison's Australia-to-England record, but then in 1931 *Southern Cross* returned to the news when Kingsford-Smith used it to rescue an experimental consignment of airmail. The Imperial Airways DH66, bringing the mail from England, force-landed on the island of Timor and was put out of action. Qantas had a contract to transport the mail from Darwin, but did not have an aircraft capable of crossing the Timor Sea with it. Kingsford-Smith came to the rescue in *Southern Cross*, not only flying out to Timor to fetch the inbound mail, but also flying the outbound mail as far as Burma, where it was transferred to Imperial Airways.

Later in the year he also rescued the Christmas mail. The Australian National Airways Avro Ten, *Southern Sun*, broke down on Alor Star in Malaya, taking the Christmas mail to Great Britain. Kingsford-Smith set off in another Avro Ten to retrieve the situation.

Once more he encountered a storm over northern Australia and landed in Darwin amidst thunder and lightning. On the soft ground the aircraft crashed into a telegraph pole and was severely damaged. Frantic repairs put it back into the air and he was able to proceed to Alor Star and collect the mail. He then flew to England through fog and snowstorms, arriving in time on 16 December, and saving the reputation of his airline.

Nevertheless, Kingsford-Smith's fortunes were to plummet again, and in 1932 he was reduced to giving joy-flights in *Southern Cross* at 10 shillings a flip. The following year he once more broke the England-to-Australia record, this time flying a Percival Gull, which he named *Miss Southern Cross*. He was once more a national hero, knighted by the King, and granted £3000 by a proud Government.

Perhaps Australia is the only country where heroes are knocked off their pedestals with greater alacrity than England, and Kingsford-Smith was to discover this one more time. He naturally entered for the England-to-Australia air race of 1934. With money raised by public subscription, he purchased a Lockheed Altair for the race, but when the aircraft was badly damaged in Australia it was not possible to repair it in time to reach England for the start. He was the victim of much approbation, and determined to return the aircraft to its makers.

With PG Taylor as co-pilot he flew from Australia to America across the Pacific, becoming the first man to do so, just as he had been the first to make the flight in the opposite direction. His place on the pedestal was assured. He was unable to sell the Altair, and had it shipped to Great Britain.

He made his last flight in the old *Southern Cross* on 18 July 1935 from Mascot to Richmond, where he handed it over to the people of Australia. There it remained in storage until 1944, when RAAF fitters put it back together again for use in a film about Kingsford-Smith's life. This famous aircraft was then installed in a purpose-built building at Eagle Farm Airport, Brisbane, very near to the point Kingsford-Smith completed his Pacific flight.

Later in 1935 Sir Charles Kingsford-Smith set out on his last flight from England to Australia in the Altair *Lady Southern Cross*, with co-pilot Thomas Pethybridge. They left Lympne on 6 November, and Baghdad was reached in 29.5 hours. He was last seen on 7 November flying over Calcutta at 21.06 hrs. He disappeared without trace over the Bay of Bengal.

Two years later a Lockheed Altair wheel was washed up on the coast of Burma. Sir Charles Kingsford-Smith was only 38 years old when he died. He had pioneered some of the great air routes of the world, and made a whole continent air-minded. He was a brave and skilful pilot, and earned all the plaudits he received.

CHAPTER 8

Down in an Ornamental Lake

Pilots flying landplanes over the sea have always been anxious not to have to make a forced landing on the water. Conversely, flying boat pilots flying over land can run into equally worrying problems. When, suddenly, that sickening moment occurs, when the engine note drops, or something breaks, they look round desperately for a piece of water, any piece of water, even an ornamental lake.

In 1935 No. 209 Squadron at Felixstowe was suffering from a lack of aircraft. They had a few old Southamptons and were able to cadge the odd flight in a Perth. To add insult to injury they became involved in the re-equipment of No. 230 Squadron, which had reformed at Pembroke Dock on 1 December 1934. They received their first Singapore III, K4579, flown directly from Short Bros at Rochester to Pembroke Dock, on 26 April 1935; the next, K4580, was collected from Rochester on 21 May; and the third, K4578, was collected on 22 June. The fourth and fifth Singapores did not arrive until August.

The Singapore III was a development of the earlier Singapore II, which though nominally a development of the much earlier Singapore I, was virtually a completely new design to Spec. R.32/27. It was a four-engined biplane flying boat, with the Kestrel engines in tandem pairs, two tractors and two pushers. The prototype, N246, flew briefly for the first time on 27 March 1930. After prolonged testing the Singapore was ordered into production in August 1933, the production version being known as the Singapore III.

The aircraft had a span of 90 feet and a length of 63 feet 9 inches, with an all-up weight of 31,500 lb. The four Kestrel engines gave it a maximum speed of 140 mph, and it had a range of 1000 miles.

No. 230 Squadron was the first to form on Singapore IIIs. Its first short cruise with the aircraft was from 10 to 14 June, with K4580 and K4579, flying to Ireland. It was planned to send No. 230 to Egypt and No. 209 was detailed to help collect all the necessary equipment for service in the Middle East, at Felixstowe, before handing the aircraft back to a No. 230 Squadron crew to ferry the aircraft to its base.

On one such occasion the Singapore, K4580, was at Felixstowe being kitted out for service to the Middle East. It was collected by Flight

29. **A Short Singapore III, K4583, at Felixstowe shortly after K4580 had departed for its unscheduled visit to Hever Castle.**

Lieutenant Hill, who had been posted to No. 230 Squadron on 16 January 1935. He had assumed command of the Squadron for a while, until Wing Commander WH Dunn, arrived as CO on 23 February. Hill arrived to fetch the aircraft on 2 September and decided to set off after an early lunch. It happened to be a Wednesday, the day No. 209 had half a day off for various sports. Flying Officer Edwin Shipley was the pilot left alone in the Duty Pilot's Hut on the Front, normally a very quiet duty. Then he received an extraordinary signal from Hill.

'Have landed in ornamental lake at Hever Castle, with tailplane struts carried away in the air.'

The Singapore had been flying sedately over Kent, when the tail incidence gear failed. This was not the only known failure of these struts, before Shorts managed to cure the problem, but it gave Hill some heart-stopping moments.

He happened to be over Edenbridge in Kent. Below him were the grounds of Hever Castle, and most importantly, the 700 yard long ornamental lake. Hill successfully managed to land the aircraft, and taxied to the bank to explain his sudden arrival to the curious locals.

Although a successful landing had been made on the lake, it seemed rather too small to consider a take-off, so John Lankester Parker, the chief test pilot of Short Bros, was consulted. He was, perhaps, the most experienced flying boat pilot in the country, as he had been testing waterborne aircraft for the Royal Naval Air Service even before his employment with the country's pre-eminent flying boat manufacturers.

John Lankester Parker's family had run a flour mill at Barton Mills, Mildenhall. In 1910, aged 14 he first took a sudden interest in flying when out on a walk with his elder brother. They watched some rooks performing startling aerial manoeuvres, and the young man suddenly declared his intention of becoming a pilot, but he did not even see an aircraft for two years. In the autumn of 1912 two BE2s landed at Worlington near his home, while on Army exercises.

Lankester Parker learned to fly at the Vickers School at Brooklands and qualified in June 1914. He became a flight instructor on seaplanes at the school on Lake Windermere, and also a freelance test pilot. When he arrived at Short Bros at Eastchurch in 1916, Horace Short would not at first let him test any aircraft, believing him too young, but Lankester Parker persisted. In the end Horace Short relented and told him to test fly a Short bomber. He actually put three of the Short bombers through their tests that day, and became Shorts' chief test pilot, a position he held for over thirty years.

Lankester Parker travelled the short distance to Hever Castle to examine the problem. At the same time Short Bros sent a team out to undertake temporary repairs to the aircraft, which took until 13 September. Normally, when an aircraft is flown out of a restricted space the technique is to hold the brakes on, while the engines are run up to full power and then release them. Flying boats, of course, have no brakes. Lankester Parker ordered the Singapore to be lightened as much as was possible, and then had it tethered to a very stout tree. He took just one other crew member aboard with him, a fitter named Corporal Lewis, who was sited in the rear gunner's position, armed with an axe. Lankester Parker ran up the engines to full throttle, and then signalled the fitter to chop the rope. The big Singapore shot forward like a rocket, as far as such a stately flying machine could, and left the lake in almost as spectacular a fashion as it had arrived.

The aircraft was flown back to Rochester for final repairs, and was then flown back to the Squadron on 22 September, along with K4578 and K4579. After being handed back to the RAF, K4580 went with the No. 230 Squadron to the Middle East, departing on 23 September, with Wing Commander Dunn piloting. K4580 became the CO's usual aircraft.

On New Year's Day in 1936 K4580 carried out a sea search for another flying boat in trouble, the Imperial Airways Short Calcutta, G-AASJ, *City of Khartoum*. This was a veteran boat, which had flown for the first time on 10 January 1930, being handed over to Imperial Airways the following day. The Calcuttas had been withdrawn from service, but two had been pressed back into use on the Mediterranean route after the crash of the Short Kent *Sylvanus*.

In putting them back into use, a mechanic had adjusted the carburettor jets to consume 10 per cent too much fuel. Approaching the flare path at Alexandria on the evening of 31 December 1935, all three engines of *City of Khartoum* had run out of fuel and stopped together. The aircraft fell out of the air and the hull spilt open when it hit the water. It sank immediately.

The flare path crew were amazed to see the aircraft's lights suddenly disappear, but could not send the Imperial Airways tender out of the harbour as it was not built to cope with the open sea. It was some hours before the duty destroyer could get up steam and reach the area, and K4580 was also sent out on the search at first light. Sadly, only the pilot of the Calcutta was found and rescued.

No. 230 Squadron returned to the UK after this deployment on 30 July 1936. Before being deployed to the Far East, it handed over three of its Singapores, including K4580, to No. 210 Squadron. They remained with No. 210 until September 1938, when they were passed fleetingly to No. 209 Squadron. Once more No. 209 did not get its hands on K4580 for very long, as it was turned over to the ECD in October. The aircraft was then transferred to the Flying Boat Training Squadron in September 1939. It was finally struck off charge in 1940, after a far longer and more eventful career than might have been expected if that ornamental lake at Hever Castle had not hove into view at just the right moment.

CHAPTER 9

Down in the Desert and Down in the Sea

In 1936 the chief designer of General Aircraft, FF Crocombe, flew to Australia. On the way his airliner force-landed in the Arabian desert, and on the way back, just seven weeks later, he force-landed on a tidal reef in the Timor Sea.

Fred Crocombe had worked for Fairey Aviation until HJ Steiger formed the Monospar Wing Company in 1930, to develop his design for a single spar wing. Steiger, who was Swiss-born, had invented the wing while working for Wm Beardmore & Co. The basis for it was a single Warren girder spar, with the torsional loads taken up by a pyramidal system of tie rods. He claimed that this system allowed a lighter wing structure, something that might have seemed alien to Beardmore. The company was most famous for the all-metal Beardmore Inflexible, the biggest landplane yet built in this country. It was so over-weight it could transport just itself and its crew around the air with awesome majesty, but could not lift a worthwhile payload. A prototype wing was built, designated the ST-1, and exhibited at the Olympia Aero Show of 1929, but it was the swansong for Beardmore, which dropped out of the aviation business.

Steiger formed the Monospar Wing Company to continue the development of the wing, and Fred Crocombe joined him as chief designer. The Air Ministry ordered a larger wing, the ST-2, to be fitted to a Fokker F.VII/3m fuselage, and work also began on the ST-3, a little three-seat aircraft powered by two 50 hp Salmson radials. The ST-3 was registered G-AARP, and so well was it received, it prompted the company to put a four-seat version, powered by two 85 hp Pobjoy radials, and called appropriately the ST-4, into production. General Aircraft Ltd was formed in 1932 to exploit the design, and to manufacture the ST-4 at Croydon. The aircraft was now called the General Aircraft Monospar ST-4. This was followed by the ST-6 with retractable undercarriage, and the two aircraft began selling in reasonable numbers. The number of employees slowly rose to sixty-five.

In 1934 a new chief engineer, DL Hollis-Williams, also formerly of Fairey, joined the company, which was moved to Hanworth later in the year and floated on the stock market. Shortly after this Steiger resigned and Eric Gordon England was appointed managing director. He was convinced the era of modern civil aviation was approaching, no doubt inspired by the tremendous strides being made in America, and initiated the design of a ten-seat twin-engined monoplane airliner, the ST-10 Croydon. The aircraft was metal-framed but fabric-covered, and was powered by two Pratt & Whitney 450 hp Wasp Juniors, as there were no suitable British engine. The monospar wing had a large degree of sweepback to balance the centre of gravity, as it was attached well forward on the fuselage to give the rudder a greater degree of moment to ease single-engined operation. Unusually, there were two over-wing bracing struts, and the siting of the wing relative to the fuselage meant that the structural bulkhead to support these struts could be sited immediately behind the cockpit, giving an unobstructed cabin for ten people, particularly so as there was no second spar to pass through the cabin.

The top speed was a very respectable 203 mph at 5000 feet, with a suggested cruising speed of 190 mph at 75 per cent power. The range was 600 miles, and the asking price was £8000. Built at Hanworth, the Croydon was a very modern design in many respects, with a retractable undercarriage, Dowty hydraulic units and two-blade variable pitch propellers. Because of the noisy nature of the Wasp Junior, there was extensive soundproofing in the cabin. Behind the cabin there was a 41 cubic feet luggage compartment. Despite being very fast and modern in comparison with contemporary British airliners, the Croydon suffered in comparison with American aircraft by not being of all-metal stressed skin construction, and British Airways preferred to order the Lockheed 10.

Registered G-AECB, the Croydon made its first flight in March 1936, having taken only ten months to construct. Despite British Airways turning it down, sales prospects looked good in Australia, where Oceanic Airways operated ten Monospar four-seaters. Major CR Anson of Anson Airways offered to buy G-AECB as his personal aircraft, if it made a record-breaking flight to Australia. General Aircraft did not really wish to part with the Croydon just yet, but saw the flight to Australia as an excellent way to demonstrate the aircraft's capabilities to potential customers.

The flight was planned with a crew of four. Lord Sempill was to be in charge of the flight and act as second pilot, with Harold 'Timber' Wood as chief pilot. Captain Wood was very experienced, and had been the chief pilot of Hillman Airways, until becoming Major Anson's pilot. The other two crew were Gilroy the wireless operator and Davies the ground engineer.

Two extra fuel tanks, with a capacity totalling 40 gallons, were fitted but there were no other modifications. It was intended to operate the aircraft as if it were a normal airline flight, to prove the Croydon's capabilities. They took off from Croydon, appropriately, on 30 July with attendant publicity. The first part of the flight went well, flying via Vienna, Athens, Aleppo, Bushire and Jask on the Persian Coast of the Gulf of Oman, but that is where things started going wrong.

After leaving Jask for Karachi they encountered bad weather and were forced to turn back. Lord Sempill made a very heavy landing and damaged the tailwheel. A temporary repair enabled them to reach Karachi, but closer inspection there showed much greater structural damage than first suspected.

30. Lord Sempill (left) and Harold 'Timber' Wood, about to start on their flight to Australia.

Fred Crocombe flew out to supervise repairs, taking the first available Imperial Airways flight. Unfortunately, the Imperial Airways schedule was badly disrupted when the Short Kent flying boat *Scipio* landed heavily in Mirabella Bay on 22 August and sank. On 28 August Crocombe boarded the Handley Page HP42 G-AAUC, *Horsa* at Kisumu to take him on to Karachi, but the captain felt the pressure to make up time. After refuelling at Basra on 28 August, he took off again at 22.30 hrs for Bahrain, without ensuring that Bahrain Station had been informed, perhaps because he had already been on duty for 18 hours. Bahrain did not light up, and with no moon the pilot was unable to find the island and overshot by 100 miles. These days the eastern coast of Saudi Arabia is a flood of light, not least from the many gas flares, but also with wide well-lit dual carriageways and brightly lit towns. In 1936 there were no roads in the eastern province of Saudi Arabia, and no electricity. The first oil well was not drilled until the following year. *Horsa* would have been travelling over dark, featureless desert or sea.

Finding themselves over barren desert at first light, and running short of fuel, they attempted a landing, but the starboard undercarriage leg collapsed. None of the four crew or nine passengers, who included one woman, the American authoress Jane Smith, were injured, and they settled down under the port wing to wait for possible rescue.

When it was realised that *Horsa* was missing the Royal Air Force began to organise a search and rescue operation. Six Vickers Vincents of No. 84 Squadron took off from Shaibah in Iraq before dawn, to operate a search from Bahrain. The Vincent was a general purpose version of the Vildebeest torpedo-bomber. With a large fuel tank where the Vildebeest's torpedo had been, the Vincent had a range of 1250 miles, and a reliable 635 hp Bristol Pegasus engine, so it was ideal for long searches. At 06.00 hrs a Vickers Valentia, J8921, of No. 70 Squadron followed from Hinaidi. The Valentia was the final development of the Victoria biplane transport, with Bristol Pegasus radials replacing the Victoria's Napier Lions. It also had a beefed-up structure, which enabled it to carry twenty-two fully equipped troops; though it was rather slow, managing only 120 mph at 5000 ft. The Valentia had a five-man crew: Pilot Officer C Fothergill; Pilot Officer W Locker; AC1 Wyse, the wireless operator; Corporal Tyler and LAC Andrews. They landed at Shaibah and then Basra to pick up Group Captain W Calloway, Wing Commander A Briscoe and two medical orderlies. As they flew south they searched the Arabian coast from Mina Abu Ali to Bahrain, where they landed at 17.30 hrs. The six Vincents had searched but failed to find *Horsa*, landing back at Bahrain for the night. A second Valentia was ordered to Bahrain, to be equipped for supply dropping.

The Armament Staff at Hinaidi worked all night to get Valentia K1311 ready, and it took off at 06.00 hrs, piloted by Flying Officer IHD Walker. He landed at Shaibah at 09.00 hrs to pick up further stores and personnel. Then, loaded to the maximum 19,100 lb, he took off for Bahrain at 10.20 hrs.

Meanwhile, Flight Lieutenant HR Bardon, the OC of 'C' Flight, No. 84 Squadron had located *Horsa* at 08.00 hrs. It was about 100 miles south of Bahrain near to a place called Salwah Wells, at the base of what would now be called the Qatar Peninsula. It was very near to the present-day Saudi Arabian border, though in those times borders were ill-defined and largely ignored by the locals. With two other Vincents Bardon located a suitable landing ground about one and a half miles away from *Horsa*, he landed, and marked out an airstrip for the Valentias.

Pilot officer Fothergill in his Valentia left Bahrain at 10.45 hrs and reached the landing ground at 12.50 hrs. With members of his crew he then

31. **(Above) The HP42 *Horsa* after it's forced landing in the desert, with the passengers and crew sheltering from the fierce heat under a wing.**

32. **(Right) The collapsed starboard undercarriage of *Horsa*.**

walked to *Horsa*, where he found the crew and passengers sheltering from the fierce heat of the midday sun under the wing. Jane Smith was reputed to be only wearing her cami-knickers, a garment she later autographed and presented to her rescuers! The passengers were all exhausted and needed considerable persuasion to leave the shade to set off across the featureless desert to walk to the Valentia. However in the end they drank the last of their water, about a cupful each, and set off. The captain and steward insisted on staying.

Even after a few yards, walking in the midday sun in the Gulf leaves one drenched in sweat, yet the sun burns all exposed skin. The temperature in the shade can reach 140°F in August, and away from the broad wings of the HP42 there was no shade. An even worse ordeal is the humidity experienced near to the Gulf coast. Further inland, in conditions of almost zero humidity, even 140°F is tolerable, but in high humidity, the body dehydrates rapidly, and rivulets of sweat pour constantly down. The summer heat and humidity of the Gulf is among the fiercest climates in the world.

Before leaving, Fothergill sent 4 gallons of water back to *Horsa*. After a total of 6 miles walking in those conditions, one of the crew collapsed on the way back and had to be assisted. Fothergill took off at 15.30 hrs. local time and reached Bahrain at 17.35 hrs.

Meanwhile, Flying Officer Walker had taken off from Bahrain in K1311 at 14.35 hrs, arriving at the landing ground at 16.35 hrs. The crew walked to *Horsa*, where they found the captain and steward, who were still adamant they wished to remain. The Valentia crew carried 150 lb of mail back to the landing ground, and after take-off dropped one container of water and one of food by the stricken airliner. Fothergill landed back at Bahrain at 20.10 hrs, after a total of 10 hours 25 minutes of flying, without a proper break or food.

On 31 August both Valentias left for Salwah Wells at 08.30 hrs, and on arrival set up a ground WT Station at the landing ground. They fetched two loads of mail from *Horsa*, and then the medical officer forbade any further such work. This time they had taken a political officer, and he insisted on the captain and steward leaving. On arrival in Bahrain, the steward had to be admitted to hospital.

On 1 September the two Valentias flew back to the landing ground, taking an engineering officer of No. 203 Squadron, a Singapore III unit, and a sergeant rigger and AC fitter of No. 55 Squadron, a Wapiti unit. They also took fourteen 'coolies' who carried all the remaining mail, the baggage and personal effects. During this operation AC Wyse collapsed and was sent back to Basra to be hospitalised.

On 2 September the two Valentias returned to Iraq, J8921 arriving at Basra after a total of 25 hours 35 minutes flying and K1311 at Shaibah after 26 hours 50 minutes flying. *Horsa* was eventually repaired and flown out from a prepared runway. It continued to serve the Middle East run, until impressed into RAF service during the War. It survived until 7 August 1940, when *en route* from Ringway to Stornoway it force-landed at Moresby Park, Cumberland, caught fire and burnt out.

Fred Crocombe, meanwhile, continued his ill-fated journey to Karachi, where with the help of the Imperial Airways ground staff he undertook repairs to the ST-10 Croydon. Lord Sempill had been forced to return to England on pressing business, and so Crocombe decided to take his place on the resumed flight to Australia, taking off on 11 September, with 'Timber' Wood as the sole pilot.

They flew via Jodhpur and Allahabad to Calcutta, cruising at 75 per cent power, and yet managing a respectable average speed of 191.6 mph with a following wind. They then set off for Rangoon but flew into a frightening monsoon storm over the Bay of Bengal. The weather report had been promising, and they were cruising comfortably at 4000 feet through light cloud when suddenly they flew into a cloud front, which became a solid wall of water. The Croydon was flung about the sky like a toy, and Gilroy and Davies both hit the roof before they managed to strap themselves in. Crocombe, sitting in the co-pilot's seat, was horrified as he watched the altimeter recording huge changes of altitude as the aircraft was flung up and then down. Rarely has an aircraft's designer had to rely so heavily on his own calculations. Wood was often unable to say which way up the aircraft was pointing, as the instruments contradicted one another, and the seat of his pants told him something else entirely. A glance back into the cabin revealed the ashen faces of Davies and Gilroy praying for an end to it. After

33. The ST-10 Croydon after resuming its journey, at one of the stops in India.

45 minutes of this ordeal they emerged with much relief in calm air, glad to be in one piece. Fred Crocombe was to observe that, 'Anyway we learnt that the cockpit and cabin were waterproof, that the wing tips did not advertise the severe bumps unduly, and that it was not difficult to keep dead on course in bad conditions.' He added, 'Naturally the longitudinal and lateral disturbances took some looking after !'

They reached Rangoon having averaged 186.5 mph, despite the storm. The flight continued via Penang, Batavia, Sourabaya and Koepang, and then over the Timor Sea to Darwin. Most of the flight in the tropics was carried out at 10,000 feet, which was sometimes quite cold after the extreme heat they found on the ground.

'Timber' Wood was often able to fly the plane with just a touch of the rudder bias now and then to keep on course. If the others did not move around in the cabin, he was also often able to fly hands-off as well. To keep him awake, and to relieve the boredom, Wood was kept going with a constant supply of coffee and cigarettes. Over the Timor Sea they had a problem with the compass, which appeared to be reading 10 degrees out, a problem that was to have drastic consequences later.

They then crossed Australia via Daly Waters, Brunette Downs, Cloncurry and Charleville to Melbourne. Over Australia the air was very bumpy, and Wood was not able to relax quite so much, especially as navigation was very difficult over the unmapped expanses of the outback.

Unfortunately, because they had not broken the record, Major Anson would not buy the Croydon, but they undertook a number of demonstrations, including flying from Melbourne to Sydney in only 2.5 hours. In contrast, Crocombe took 15 hours on the train in returning. They also took part in the Victoria Air Pageant on 26 September and won the Herald Cup with the fastest time.

They decided to attempt to break the record for the homeward flight, because they knew the aircraft was capable of it, even at 75 per cent power. They flew from Melbourne to Darwin on 6 October, taking off from

Essendon well before dawn and arriving just as the sun set, having averaged 188.4 mph. Although their agents in Melbourne, Robert Bryce & Co., had arranged with the authorities to telegraph Darwin with news of their flight, they only did this when it was too late to contact Koepang, which had gone off the air. They intended to take-off for Koepang early in the morning, but as they knew that there was a Qantas flight due in from Ranbang just after dawn, they assumed the Koepang W/T operator would be on duty in time to give them bearings. This was important because they had only been able to contact Darwin W/T when just 80 miles away, and they were still unsure of their compass.

On the outward journey there had been an increased deviation the further east they flew, rising to a maximum 10 degrees over the Timor Sea. The compass had been found correct at Melbourne, and had not deviated as they approached Darwin, but they were still worried, and did not wish to rely on it. They hoped to take back bearings from Darwin, until Koepang came on the air to give them bearings.

They took off for Koepang at 04.47 hrs the following morning using a flare path, and flew out to sea in the darkness on a compass course of 282 degrees, allowing for drift and magnetic variation; the true course for Koepang being 287 degrees. After 25 minutes they received their first back bearing from Darwin of 288 degrees, indicating that they were 1 degree north of track. Wood changed course to 280 degrees for 20 minutes, hoping to come back on line, but to their surprise the next back bearing still showed them north of their intended track.

They suspected the compass was playing up again, as the weather seemed to indicate that their drift was negligible. To get back on track, Wood turned 5 degrees south, the compass course being 275 degrees. Twenty minutes later they received another bearing from Darwin and were perplexed when it was given as 289 degrees, indicating that they were still north of the intended track. For the first time, they suspected the bearings and Wood asked Gilroy to make a further check. He was told by Darwin that the bearing was 'first class', or plus or minus 1 degree. They were further puzzled that the compass error seemed to be opposite to the one they had experienced on the outward journey. They decided that they had to trust the back bearings from Darwin, as the W/T operator there was so confident of them, and Wood turned to a course of 270 degrees and flew for another 30 minutes, only to be told their bearing was still one degree north of track.

It was now 06.33 hrs, and their ETA at Koepang was 07.15 hrs, so Wood decided not to make any more course changes, as a 1 degree change so near their destination would not make much difference. In any case, with Koepang situated at the western end of the island of Timor, if they were north of track they would be sure to strike land, and could then fly down the coast to find the landing ground.

By 06.40 hrs their signal was so weak Darwin was unable to give bearings, and they could not contact Koepang. Wood descended through the haze to 3000 feet in the hope of sighting land. At 08.00 hrs, already 45 minutes overdue, they sighted a circular reef. They thought this indicated the nearness of land and began searching mainly to the north of the reef, but saw only two more reefs. Gilroy was trying to contact anyone on the wireless, hoping to check the location of the reefs, but could no longer even raise Darwin.

By 09.00 hrs their fuel was getting critically low. They had started with 235 gal, and had a normal consumption of 45 gal/hr, which gave them a duration of 5.22 hours. At the northernmost reef they saw a fishing boat. After dropping a can near to it asking for directions, and getting no response, they decided to attempt a landing. With only about one hour's fuel left, and no indication in which direction land lay, except their instinct that it was to the north, they did not wish to take the risk of landing in the sea, even though they did carry a collapsible boat.

At 09.15 hrs. after winding in the aerial, Wood made an approach with the wheels down, just touching the surface, which seemed solid but covered with a layer of sea water. They strapped in tightly, Gilroy and Davies in the cabin, and Wood came in once more. Crocombe put the flaps half down and Wood came smoothly in executing a fine three-point landing and pulling up quickly to avoid some scattered groups of boulders, apparently avoiding damage. Seeing what seemed to be slightly higher ground further on, he began to taxi forward. However, then the tailwheel fell through the coral and there was a loud crack, and the tail dipped, the elevator control going soggy.

Switching off, they clambered out and examined the aircraft. The tailwheel had fallen through the surface crust of coral and the yoke was broken. Wood had hoped they might get fuel to the reef and take off again, but now there seemed no possibility of that. They were about 10 yards from the west side of the reef, where the coral dropped steeply away and large waves were breaking. Fred Crocombe was once more stranded by an airliner with a broken undercarriage in inhospitable surroundings, as he had been seven weeks before. Apart from the heat, however, his situation could hardly be more different.

They wound out the aerial using the oars of their collapsible boat to hold it aloft, but though they could hear Darwin and Koepang, they could not contact them. As they were overdue, all shipping in the area had been alerted, but they had force-landed on Seringapatam Reef well to the west of their intended track and so immediate rescue was unlikely.

In an attempt to improve transmission and to recharge the battery, which was running down, Wood started the port engine, which was equipped with a generator. By 11.15 hrs they were resigned to the fact that they were out of range of all W/T stations. It was now abundantly clear that the tide was coming in, so they contacted the fishing boat and were taken off. The only word the fishermen understood was 'Koepang' and when SS *Nimoda* came across them, and took them on board, that is just where the fishermen had been heading – without the dubious aid of compasses or back bearings !

They had landed on the reef on one of the three days per month when it was uncovered. At high tide the same day it was covered to a depth of 3 feet. Later in the month it was covered by 14 feet, so that was the end of the Croydon, which had had a brief but adventurous existence. Crocombe had to admit, 'One of the hardest things I have ever had to do was to leave the

34. (Above) The ST-10 Croydon after its forced landing on the reef.

35. (Left) The crew of the Croydon examining their supplies shortly after landing.

aircraft stranded, through no fault of its own, standing up like a monument in the clear atmosphere until the sea eventually claimed it'.

Seringapatam Reef was 600 miles from Darwin on a bearing of 262 degrees, which indicated a compass error of 15 degrees. Koepang was 267 miles away, so they would not have been able to reach it even on a direct route from the reef, and the nearest W/T station was Broome on the Australian coast, 300 miles away.

An investigation into the affair by the Australian authorities placed most of the blame on the shoulders of the Darwin W/T personnel. Owing to the error known as 'Night Effect' they should not have allowed Wood to rely on bearings given during darkness, and especially around sunrise, something the pilot should have known as well. In particular, the W/T operator should not have stated that his bearings were 'first class', as the report states '. . .when they were most certainly not of any class at all'.

Fred Crocombe had been rescued unharmed twice from forced landings in the space of seven weeks, once from the desert and once from the sea, surviving a monsoon storm in between. He went back to General Aircraft where his designs included the Hamilcar glider and the Universal Freighter, which became the Blackburn Beverley when the company was taken over by

Blackburn. 'Timber' Wood became General Aircraft's chief test pilot, and made the first flight of the Universal Freighter. Having seen the Beverley into production, Crocombe left Blackburn & General Aircraft and joined Boulton Paul Aircraft as chief designer. He was later to give talks on his many adventures back in 1936, when he flew to Australia and back, the hard way.

36. The rescuers; the fishermen who picked up the Croydon's crew from the reef.

CHAPTER 10

Down in the Channel

Since Hubert Latham failed to make the first flight over the English Channel in his Antoinette monoplane in 1909, there have been many pilots who have come down in that short stretch of water. Even pilots who survived the ditching have found that being so close to two shores does not always mean rescue is at hand, especially bomber crews flying on dark nights during the Second World War, in either direction. However, 31 May 1940 was a good day to ditch in the Channel, because on that day there was a stream of boats and ships crossing and recrossing those narrow waters on their way to and from Dunkirk. It was on that day that Eric Barwell's Merlin engine stopped, and he had to put his Boulton Paul Defiant down on the water.

At the time Barwell was a pilot officer with No. 264 Squadron, one of two Defiant squadrons then in existence, but the only one yet to see action. No. 264 (Madras Presidency) Squadron had been re-formed at Sutton Bridge on 30 October 1939, and was destined to become the first squadron equipped with the new Boulton Paul Defiant, though the first three did not arrive until 9 December.

The Defiant had been designed to Spec. F.9/35, calling for a two-seat fighter with all its armament in a fully-enclosed power-operated gun turret, as a replacement for the Hawker Demon biplane. Boulton Paul Aircraft had designed an aircraft that was an excellent compromise between simplicity of construction and aerodynamic efficiency. More modern in construction than the fabric-covered Hurricane, and yet easier to build in simple sub-assemblies than the Spitfire, it was in some ways a shame it was designed for a specification that called for it to haul around 850 lb of gunner and gun turret, unlike the other two, similarly-powered, monoplane fighters being prepared for service with the Royal Air Force. Even

37. Eric Barwell in 1941, the year after he ditched his Defiant in the Channel.

with the turret its performance came remarkably close to that of the Hurricane, achieving in excess of 300 mph.

Eric Barwell was a member of the RAFVR from early June 1938, doing his part-time elementary flying training at No. 22 E & RFTS at Cambridge. He was called up at the start of the War and went to No. 2 FTS at Brize Norton on 8 October 1939. He was commissioned as a pilot officer on 10 December and was advised that he was to be posted to No. 266 Squadron at Sutton Bridge, flying Spitfires. However that station was commanded by his brother, Wing Commander Phillip Barwell, and they both agreed that this was not a good arrangement and so his posting was switched to No. 264 Squadron, flying Defiants at Martlesham Heath.

He drove to Martlesham Heath on 20 December and reported to Squadron Leader Stephen Hardy, who advised him that he ought to have more training first, possibly because of his RAFVR status. He went home for Christmas and reported to No. 12 Group Fighter Pool at Aston Down on 1 January 1940. He had a month of flying Harvards and then returned to No. 264 Squadron during the first week in February.

He was taken aloft by Flight Lieutenant Nicholas Cooke, in command of A Flight, in a Magister. He then had two flights in a Fairey Battle, followed by a trip in the gun turret of a Defiant being piloted by Cooke. After that he was deemed proficient enough to be let loose on the Defiant, which he soon got used to and enjoyed flying. During his first month he flew about 8 hours, which included firing at targets in the Wash, formation flying and attack practices. During March Squadron Leader Phillip Hunter replaced Hardy. He set about devising tactics to use the unique features of the Defiant and to weld each two-man crew into a well-drilled team.

During this period the Squadron could almost have been operating in peacetime, but their leisurely progress was rudely jarred when the Germans launched their invasion of Holland and Belguim. On 12 May Barwell, with his gunner Sergeant Quinnie, was one of six crews detailed to fly a mission to Holland in the company of six Spitfires from No. 66 Squadron. During the operation the Squadron shot down a Junkers Ju 88, and all returned successfully.

The following day B Flight flew a similar operation but were attacked by large numbers of Bf 109s. In a terrific battle the Defiants shot down three Bf 109s and four Ju 87s, but only one of their number made it back to Duxford. One of the Defiants made a belly-landing on Dutch soil, so that the Germans were able to examine the aircraft and find out all about its unique armament.

The next day Barwell set off with A Flight on a similar mission, but they were recalled after take-off. Holland had surrendered.

They then had a week of practice flying, including dummy attacks on a Wellington bomber. Barwell changed his gunner, and now had Pilot Officer JEM Williams, known as Bruce or Willie, who was an ex-stunt man, and had done over 500 parachute drops at air shows. Six replacement Defiants and replacement aircrew also arrived.

From 23 May they flew to Manston, were refuelled and brought to readiness. Each day they flew two patrols along the French coast, and for the rest of the time were sitting on the ground ready to scramble. By 26 May the British Expeditionary Force was confined in the Dunkirk pocket, with the Belgiam Army to the North about to disintegrate.

On 27 May No. 264 Squadron flew a patrol over the Dunkirk area, without Barwell, and intercepted a force of twelve Heinkel He 111s. They broke up the formation and claimed three shot down and two damaged. The Defiant had proven itself in the role of which it had been designed, as a bomber destroyer. The following day ten Defiants set off from Manston, but about halfway across the Channel they were attacked by around thirty Bf 109s.

Squadron Leader Hunter adopted the defensive tactic he had devised and put the Defiants into a defensive circle. Three Defiants were lost, but they claimed five German fighters, and had shown that they could at least defend themselves against superior numbers of single-seat fighters.

Eric Barwell's next action was on the following day, the most auspicious in the history of No. 264 Squadron, and the Defiant. He and Williams were

38. Pilot Officer JEM 'Bruce' Williams, Eric Barwell's gunner at the time of the ditching.

in one of the twelve Defiants that took off on the afternoon patrol. Immediately after take-off they could see the smoke billowing forth from the burning oil tanks at Dunkirk. The Squadron soon found itself in a fiece air

39. A group of No. 264 squadron Defiant gunners at the time of Dunkirk. Pilot Officer JEM 'Bruce' Williams, Barwell's gunner when he ditched, is seated fourth from the left in the front row.

40. No. 264 squadron, A Flight, on patrol, just before Dunkirk.

battle over Dunkirk, and such confusion that it was difficult to remain in formation as battle took place all over the sky.

Barwell found himself amongst a number of Bf 109s. Williams fired at several, but they were only able to claim one as destroyed, which they saw going down trailing smoke and hitting the sea. The Squadron as a whole claimed eight Bf 109s, nine Bf 110s and a Junkers Ju 87, for the loss of just one gunner, LAC Jones, who had baled out, his turret having been hit. He had presumably mistaken his pilot's violent evasive action for the aircraft being out of control. Not surprisingly, they were cock-a-hoop, and once the aircraft had been refuelled and rearmed they were chomping at the bit, anxious to return to the battle.

41. No. 264 Squadron Defiant crew at the time of Dunkirk. Left to right 'Bruce' Williams, Kay, Hackwood, Whitley, Stokes, Squadron Leader Hunter (CO), Thomas, Hickman, Young, Lauder, Barwell.

They were not sent over the Channel until the evening, however, and this time they were able to attack a large number of Junkers Ju 87s, which had just arrived to dive-bomb the beaches. Barwell attacked one, and it exploded as Williams opened fire. Barwell then joined up with two other Defiants and flew in rough line abreast through then gaps between four Ju 87s. All four exploded almost at once as the gunners poured fire into the central fuel tanks under the pilot and gunner.

As a whole, the Squadron claimed eighteen Junkers Ju 87s and a single Ju 88 on the evening sortie, with no loss to themselves. This made a total of thirty-seven claimed for the day, with none of their own aircraft shot down, a record for Fighter Command.

The Squadron landed at Manston, refuelled, and then took off to return to their base at Duxford. *En route*, Squadron Leader Hunter heard that the weather was not too good at Duxford, and as it was getting late, ordered a return to Manston. Coming in to land, Barwell realised that he was overshooting, but being exhausted both mentally and physically by the day's efforts he decided not to go round, but to try and land, believing there was enough runway beyond the top of Manston's hill. Just over the top there was a road, and he went straight over this and ended up in a potato field with a bent undercarriage strut. To compound matters he had left his radio on 'transmit', and so could not hear Hunter trying to tell him to go round again.

That night Barwell stayed at Manston, and the next day flew a Miles Master back to Duxford, the Squadron having been released from operations for the day.

On 31 May they flew to Manston and were brought to readiness while the aircraft were being refuelled. At around lunchtime they were ordered to patrol over Dunkirk docks. Barwell was the leader of Green Section, and he saw a great deal of activity on the ground and in the air. Hunter led the squadron to attack around twenty He 111s approaching from the south-east, with an escort of about seventy Bf 109s, but as they attacked the Heinkels turned and ran, and the Bf.109s swept in to attack the Defiants.

Barwell saw his number two, Pilot Officer Hickman, shoot down a German fighter, but Hickman's plane was then hit, and fell away with smoke pouring from it. Both Hickman and his gunner, LAC Fidler, managed to bale out. Williams called 'Fighters astern!', and tracer shells shot past Barwell's port side. He turned violently to starboard, and Williams opened fire at the attacking Bf 109. After a short burst the German aircraft caught fire and fell into the sea.

The sky was full of twisting aircraft, and Barwell watched in horror as a Defiant dropped in four pieces: the centre-section, turret, aft fuselage and tail. The aircraft was that of Pilot Officer Young and his gunner LAC Johnson, who had just shot down a Bf 109, and were then hit by the violently turning Defiant of Pilot Officer 'Bull' Whitley and his gunner LAC Turner. Whitley's propeller cut off the tail of Young's Defiant, which caused it to disintegrate, but he was able to crash-land his own aircraft at Dunkirk, and was soon back with the squadron.

The Squadron flew back to Manston and were soon back on readiness.

Barwell's gunner, Williams, accidentally inflated his Mae West from the CO^2 bottle, and forgot to replace the bottle, something that was nearly cost him his life a few hours later. In the late afternoon they were sent back over Dunkirk, where they found the sky full of German bombers and fighters. Barwell had a couple of fleeting engagements with fighters, and then came upon a solitary Heinkel He 111, which he attacked. Williams gave it a long burst of around 100 rounds, which entered the underside of the cabin, after which the bomber dived away towards the sea, and they saw two parachutes.

They then attacked a Vee formation of three Heinkels. They again fired into the underside, but this time with no apparent effect, apart from return fire from the bomber's gunner. Suddenly, there was a 'whoosh!' and the cockpit filled with steam. Barwell concluded that a round had hit the coolant system, and he throttled back. Williams gave another 30-round burst at three other Heinkels that came into range. Barwell jettisoned the cockpit canopy to clear the steam and headed for the Kent coast, trying to maintain their 7500 feet altitude on minimum revs. However, it seemed unlikely that they would make it back to dry land.

Barwell asked Williams whether he thought they should bale out or try and ditch, but the gunner left it up to his pilot, which was perhaps surprising in view of his extensive experience as a parachutist. Barwell decided to ditch, as there was a constant stream of boats below them, which would be more likely to pick them up if they ditched alongside, than if they drifted any distance under their parachutes.

Slowly the oil temperature went off the dial, and the engine began to slow down until it was only going at a fast tick-over despite the throttle being fully forward. Barwell examined the various boats below, trying to decide which to choose. There were pleasure cruisers, but they seemed rather small. There were fishing boats, but he decided not to choose one of those as he thought they would be rather smelly. He was very lucky to be able to make such an irrelevant choice, many an airman ditching in the Channel over the next few years would have been more than a little grateful to be able to put down alongside any sort of boat!

Then he saw two destroyers steaming in opposite directions and about a mile apart. He decided that if he ditched between them, one of them would have the decency to pick them up. He then had to decide how he was going to ditch. The standard instructions for a single-engined aircraft like the Defiant was to keep the flaps up, to stop the nose digging in, and for the pilot to have his straps as tight as he could so as not to be thrown against the instrument panel and windscreen and rendered unconcious.

Barwell decided against the latter, as the Defiant only had a Perspex windscreen, not bullet-proof glass, and no gunsight on which to hit his head, of course, so he was fairly confident that his head would survive any collision. He therefore undid his Sutton harness and parachute straps, and told Williams to point his guns forward and open the doors of his turret, which was standard procedure for Defiant gunners when landing or taking off, in case of accident. He also told him to sit on the fuselage with only his legs inside, which definitely was not standard procedure.

Barwell then sat on the back of his seat, and bent forward to hold the stick, which in the Defiant was actually attached to the seat, making this rather easier. He flew the aircraft with just one hand on the stick, the other was on the top of the windscreen, bracing him. Luckily, the sea was smooth, though this made height judgement difficult. The engine seized up completely and he glided down to make a wheels-up landing.

Suddenly he found himself deep underwater. Although he had remembered to put a few puffs of air into his Mae West, he had to swim upwards for what seemed ages before he broke surface. He looked round for Williams, but he was nowhere to be seen. Then he suddenly recognised an object floating nearby as the rear of a parasuit, the special low profile parachute worn by Defiant gunners on their backs. Barwell turned Williams the right way up, and found that he was unconcious, with a deep gash on his head. His buoyancy vest did not work, because of the empty CO_2 bottle.

Just then a landing wheel from the Defiant bobbed up alongside them, showing that the aircraft had broken up. Both destroyers seemed to be stopping. Barwell started to swim towards the nearest one, towing Williams behind him. After a while as he looked round he saw that both destroyers had apparently now completely stopped a little way off, so he aimed for one, which was to turn out to be HMS *Malcolm*. Because the parasuit on Williams' back was interfering with his legs, Barwell could not use the traditional method of life-saving and had to swim on his side, holding Williams by the front of his parasuit.

As both their heads were constantly going under water he tried to blow some more air into his Mae West, but he did not have enough 'puff'. He was getting near the end of his tether, when he saw one of the destroyers moving slowly towards them. He tried to shout 'Why the bloody Hell don't you lower a boat!' but it came out as little more than a whisper. As he got near the bows, a sailor made a wonderful dive into the sea, and relieved him of Williams. He made his way to the stern where there was a scrambling net, but was too weak to climb it unaided, and the crew had to tie a rope around him and haul him up.

He was astounded that one of the first people he saw on the deck was Mike Young, whose Defiant he had seen break up earlier in the day. They had all thought he was dead. In fact, Young had taken some time to get out of the cockpit of his stricken plane and his parachute did not open until he was quite low. He had landed in a bomb-crater unhurt except for a sprained ankle, and was able to catch the first destroyer home, which happened to be HMS *Malcolm*. He had had a grandstand view of Barwell's ditching, and was able to tell him that he had stalled when about 15 feet up, unable to judge his height because of the very smooth water.

When Williams came round the first thing he saw was Mike Young standing in the doorway with the setting sun behind him. For a moment he thought he was meeting Young in the flames of hell!

One of the destroyer's officers lent Barwell a shirt and some trousers, and when he assessed his injuries he found only bruised knees and a bruised left arm, and a cut on the lip caused by the oxygen mask. After a long wait at Dover they were returned to RAF Hawkinge and later to Duxford, where he was grounded for seven days and given 48 hours' leave.

In fact, the whole Squadron, after its massive effort over Dunkirk was given the chance to recover at Duxford, and to receive replacement aircraft and crews, ready to play its part in the Battle of Britain. During this battle they were to shoot down nineteen more German aircraft for the loss of eleven Defiants. They were then reluctantly transferred to night-time operations, as the Defiants were the best British night-fighters available to counter the *Luftwaffe*'s switch to night bombing.

By the end of the year Barwell had a total score of six victories and was awarded the DFC. He had become one of a very select band of pilots, who became 'aces' without firing their guns. At night he scored another victory, as well as a probable, which he thought was 'very probable'. The following July he was posted as a flight commander to a new Defiant squadron, No. 125 (Newfoundland) Squadron. He was still with No. 125 Squadron when they converted to Beaufighters, bringing to an end his long association with Defiants, for the time being.

Eric Barwell had reached the rank of wing commader at the end of the War. He became a member of the Boulton Paul Association in 1991, one of their projects being the restoration of a Defiant, N3378. That Eric Barwell survived his ordeal was clearly because he had chosen a very good day to ditch in the Channel.

42. Personnel of No. 125 (Newfoundland) Squadron, with Flight Commander Eric Barwell (hatless) by the Defiant's prop blade.

CHAPTER 11

Down in the North Sea

The Whitley was one of the unsung heroes of Bomber Command, a mainstay of the assault on Europe during the first years of the War. Flight Sergeant Jack Owen flew thirty-three operations on Whitleys, all within a year, his entire operational career. In one he force-landed in the North Sea and was rescued, in another he crashed in northern France, and perished with his aircraft.

John Owen, more usually 'Jack', as was the custom at the time, was born in Wolverhampton, the son of John and Louie Owen, of Deansfield Road. He had a brother, Freddie, and a sister, Nora. He was a friendly, cheerful and intelligent lad, though he had quite a bad stutter. He went to Wolverhampton Grammar School and was a regular at the Central Boy's Club in Mander Street. After leaving school he went to work in the offices of the Great Western Railway at their Stafford Road Works.

In June 1940 he went along to the RAF's recruiting office with his friends Billy Adams and Jack Whitehouse. Jack himself was accepted for pilot training, Billy joined as ground crew, but Jack Whitehouse failed the medical.

Jack Owen was inducted into the RAF at Cardington, familiar to most RAF recruits in the War. He then did his initial training at No. 3 ITU at Torquay, D Flight, No. 4 Squadron. While there he asked his sister Nora to knit him a scarf, specifying dark wool, and 2 feet 6 inches long. It could be cold in the open cockpit of a RAF training aircraft.

He did his elementary flying training at No. 11 Service Flying Training School at RAF Shawbury, Shropshire, flying Miles Magisters. It was during this time that he had his first forced landing. On his first solo cross-country flight he encountered fog, and became totally lost. In a triumph of prudence over pressing on regardless, he put the Magister down in a small field, and went to look for a telephone. A more experienced pilot was sent out to fly the Magister back to base.

After his elementary training, in March 1941, he was sent on Course 23 at the RAF College Cranwell. He then moved to No. 10 Operational Training Unit at Abingdon for his advanced flying training. At the time No. 10 OTU's strength was about eighteen Avro Ansons and forty-eight, Armstrong Whitworth Whitleys. The Armstrong Whitworth Whitley was to be the aircraft he flew for all of his operational career.

The Whitley was the pioneer of the RAF's new generation of all-metal monoplane bombers, originally equipped with hand-operated gun turrets and powered by 795 hp Armstrong-Siddeley Tiger engines. Progressive improvements meant the version that Jack Owen was to fly into war was the Mark V, powered by 1145 hp Rolls-Merlin Xs, which gave it a maximum speed of 230 mph, and a cruising speed of 210 mph. In practice, however, the Whitley was usually flown on operations at speeds much slower than this. At the maximum operational height, it could usually manage about 12,000 feet, the Whitley would normally be doing a pedestrian 120 mph.

There was a normal crew of five, including two pilots. Later RAF bombers were to have a single pilot and a flight engineer. The other crew members were the navigator, or observer as they were known, a tail gunner in his Frazer-Nash FN 4 turret with four .303-inch Browning machine-guns, and a wireless-operator. The aircraft was also fitted with a power-operated Frazer-Nash FN 16 nose turret mounting one .303-inch machine-gun. The nose turret was usually operated by the wireless operator, but was of little use, as night-fighter attacks almost always came from behind or beneath. Bomb-aiming duties were carried out either by the second pilot or by the navigator, depending on the crew. The navigator's table was behind the pilot in the cockpit, and to reach the bomb-aiming position in the nose he had to make his way to the first pilot's right and then down into the nose compartment.

On 25 August 1941, Jack Owen, now a sergeant pilot, was posted to No. 10 Squadron at RAF Leeming in Yorkshire. No. 10 Squadron, 'Shiny Ten', had been formed in the First World War but disbanded in 1919. It was re-formed in 1928 as a heavy-bomber squadron, firstly with Handley Page Hyderbads, then Hinaidis, Vickers Virginias and Handley Page Heyfords. In March 1937 it had become the first Whitley squadron. It had re-equipped with the Whitley Mk. V in May 1940 and had moved to Leeming, in the Vale of York, in July 1940.

It was the policy of No. 10 Squadron to maintain four-man crews on their Whitleys, the second pilot's position on each operation being taken by new pilots, to break them in gently. Only the day after his posting, on the night of 26/27 August, Jack Owen was detailed to fly as second pilot on Sergeant Farmery's aircraft on a bombing raid on Cologne.

On 29/30 August he was again detailed as second pilot, this time on Squadron Leader Webster's aircraft, on a raid against Frankfurt. His third operation was on the night of 7/8 September, as second pilot on Sergeant Petersen's Whitley, bombing shipping in Boulogne harbour. No. 10 Squadron did not lose any aircraft on these operations.

His fourth and last operation as a second pilot in No. 10 Squadron was to be on the night of 20/21 September, flying with Sergeant Rochford. It was almost his last operation. In the briefing room the red tape across the map stretched all the way to Berlin on a route that took them from Leeming to Robin Hood's Bay, across the North Sea to landfall at Hörnum, flying to the target via Bagenkop, and returning along the same route.

Sergeant Rochford's aircraft was Z6802, coded 'ZA-P', and would be one of eight No. 10 Squadron Whitleys on the operation. Pilot Officer Openshaw was the observer, Sergeant Cleere was in the rear turret and Sergeant Howells was the wireless operator.

43. A total of 94 aircrew of No. 10 squadron in front of one of their Whitleys in 1941. Over the next month twenty-eight of these men were dead or missing.

44. Jack Owen (left) with his crew, in front of their No. 10 Squadron Whitley.

P for Peter took off at 18.37 hrs, and crossed the North Sea without trouble, but they could not identify their landfall because of cloud and haze. North-west of Berlin an extensive searchlight belt was seen, but at 23.10 hrs Sergeant Howells received an 'Abandon Operation' signal, and they turned north to the alternative target at Wismar Bay.

They bombed the port from 14,000 feet at 00.47 hrs, and several explosions were seen in the target area. Five fires were started, which were still visible 30 miles away on the return flight. Heavy anti-aircraft fire was experienced after the bombs were dropped, and the Whitley was hit twice while flying over the Wismar Seaplane Base. Whether it was Jack Owen or Pilot Officer Openshaw in the Perspex walled bomb-aimer's position, he would have probably scrambled gratefully back up to the apparently greater security of the cockpit, with more metal around them, and the wing beneath.

Flying back over the North Sea, it became apparent that they were losing fuel, and that they would probably not be able to reach the Yorkshire coastline. They were all well aware that only just over a week before on the night of 11/12 September two of No. 10 Squadron's Whitleys, returning from a raid on Warnemünde had been forced to ditch in the North Sea. Pilot Officer Hacking's crew had ditched 2 miles off Flamborough Head out of fuel, but had been picked up an hour later by HMS *Wolsey*. Pilot Officer Purvis' crew had been forced to ditch 80 miles off the east coast and all five men had perished. Rochford and his crew hoped that they would not be faced with the same risk, and would at least reach land. They almost made it, but the engines ran out of fuel only 10 miles off Withernsea.

Howells called 'Bandlor', the call-sign for Leeming and transmitted their situation and position as Rochford and Jack brought the aircraft down to a forced landing on the sea. Even without power the Whitley was an easy aircraft to land, with a relatively low landing speed, and the ditching was very successful. They deployed the rubber dinghy and clambered aboard, as P for Peter slid beneath the waves.

They bobbed about on the waves for two hours, hoping the searchers would be able to find them. Then a High Speed Launch out of Grimsby arrived and picked them up. On arrival in Grimsby they were taken to the best hotel in town for breakfast. They had not been given a change of clothes, and as they walked into the hotel Jack looked round apprehensively at the sea water that was dripping all over the hotel's nice floors. After breakfast transport arrived from Leeming to take them back to report. Some time later they were indignant when they received a bill from the hotel for the breakfast!

A few days later yet another No. 10 Squadron Whitley, Z6941, piloted by Pilot Officer Godfrey, ditched in the sea. After a raid on Stuttgart they became lost on their return and ditched in the Bristol Channel, 22 miles south-west of Milford Haven, not surprisingly out of fuel. They were picked up four and a half hours later by a launch out of Pembroke Dock.

Such frequency of losses was a feature of life at every Bomber Command squadron. During 1941 alone No. 10 Squadron lost a total of thirty-six Whitleys, plus three Halifaxes when re-equipment began in December. Of the Squadron's ninety-four Officers and aircrew, including Jack Owen, photographed in front of a Whitley in September 1941, (see page 94) twenty-eight had died or become prisoners of war over the next month, and the Whitley behind them had also been lost!

During October Jack Owen became a first pilot and was crewed up with three other sergeants. Jenkins was his observer; Howells, previously in Sergeant Rochford's crew, was the wireless operator; and Culverwell was the rear gunner. On 28 October they were briefed for their first operation together, and Sergeant Pickett was detailed as their second pilot.

The target was shipping in Le Havre and their aircraft was Whitley Z9119, ZA-C. They took off at 17.51 hrs, and found the port successfully, though there was considerable cloud and haze. They bombed from 9500 feet and hits were seen on No. 7 Dock. They landed back at Leeming at 00.12 hrs.

Their next mission was on 28 October to Cherbourg, with Sergeant Martin as second pilot. It had to be scrubbed before take-off as the intercom was found to be unserviceable. Their third was on 31 October against shipping in Dunkirk harbour, with Pilot Officer Drake as second pilot. They made landfall at Cap Griz Nes but could not find the target because of the poor visibility, even after a 27-minute search. They jettisoned their bombs in the sea and flew home.

Jack Owen's last operation with No. 10 Squadron, on the night of 7/8 November, was almost his last in every sense. In Whitley Z6979, ZA-Z, they were one of four aircraft that took off to bomb Essen. Sergeant Wiseman was the second pilot, and they took off from Leeming at 19.23 hrs. They experienced severe icing, which affected the gyro and the auto-pilot, and despite the de-icing boots with which the Whitley was equipped, their speed fell to only 90 mph. They were forced to jettison some bombs, and abandoned the operation, returning to Leeming, where they gratefully landed at 00.59 hrs. The other three aircraft managed to avoid the icing and claimed to have bombed Essen.

Later in November Jack Owen was posted to No. 138 (Special Duties) Squadron at RAF Newmarket. No. 138 Squadron had been formed from No. 1419 Flight, which had moved to Newmarket in May 1941. Since the fall of France No. 1419 Flight had been operating in support of the resistance movements that had sprung up in all the occupied countries, dropping supplies, and taking in and bringing out agents. In November 1941 the CO Wing Commander E Knowles was posted and was replaced by Wing Commander WJ Farley, who had made the first pick-up from France, landing a Lysander at night to bring out an agent. The Squadron's strength at the time was two Lysanders, one Maryland and seven Whitleys, which were used for dropping containers of supplies, and for parachuting agents, usually know as 'Joes'.

On 16 December the Squadron moved to Stradishall, by which time it had three Lysanders, twelve Whitleys and three Halifaxes. Then on 14 March 1942 it moved to RAF Tempsford, shortly to be followed by the other Special Duties Squadron, No 161. RAF Tempsford was in Bedfordshire, 9 miles north-east of Bedford, and was to remain their base for the rest of the War. It was heavily camouflaged, both literally and by a smokescreen of silence about the activities that went on there.

RAF Tempsford was to operate in a manner quite different to other RAF stations, and was to remain a very shadowy operation. Aircraft were dispatched singly, with the crews being briefed individually, so that they often did not even know which other crews were operating on the same night. The take-off times of aircraft would also sometimes be quite different depending on where in Europe they were going, and the hours of darkness that prevailed.

The barn at Gibraltar Farm, which was next to the airfield, but conveniently remote from the other buildings, was used for the packing and storage of containers, and for preparing the 'Joes', or SOE (special operations executive) agents. The preparation and filling of containers became something of a factory operation, with over 100,000 being dropped into France alone during the War, though in 1942 there were only 207 dropped. The early containers were metal cylinders about 6 feet long, which could carry up to 2 cwt. They were attached to the normal bomb racks of the aircraft. No. 138 Squadron's contribution in its 2494 sorties from RAF Tempsford was nearly 1000 agents parachuted into France and nearly 30,000 containers dropped. During this time seventy aircraft were to be lost.

Jack Owen was detailed to operate as a second pilot for some time, doing so on at least thirteen occasions. Although it is not detailed in the Squadron's Operations Record Book, it is likely that he largely occupied the second pilot's seat with the same crew, as SD Squadron crews operated more as an individual unit than in normal bomber squadrons, planning their own missions, and always operating singly. Operations were flown at low altitude with the crew usually map-reading their way across the Continent, most usually in France. Their object would usually be to find a pre-arranged remote field, where a 'reception committee' would hopefully be waiting to flash a light, giving the correct code letter, with a series of four lights laid out in an 'L' shape showing the wind direction. Despite the fact that they stooged about the Continent only on moonlit nights, at low altitude, the Special Duties Squadron aircraft were surprisingly unmolested by the German defences.

Nevertheless, there were losses, usually due to other causes. On 29 January 1941 Sergeant Gold's Whitley came down in the sea, all seven crew on board being killed. The Whitleys often took extra men as dispatchers, dropping the large packages that were often carried in addition to the containers in the bomb-bay. These were dropped through the hole in the Whitley's floor, which was used by the parachutists, and had originally been intended for a ventral gun turret. These extra dispatchers were usually drawn from the ground crew, who were not slow to volunteer. On 10 March a Whitley, Z9125, with a complete Czech crew crashed on take-off from Stradishall.

Jack Owen was finally given command of his own crew at the end of March, on the same day as Pilot Officer Kingsford-Smith, the nephew of Sir Charles Kingsford-Smith, whose flying career is described in Chapter 7.

Jack's first operation as first pilot was on the night of 24/25 March 1942 in Whitley Z9282, on an operation code-named *Periwig*. They crossed the French Coast at Le Crotoy, at the mouth of the Somme River, a favourite landfall, at 21.28 hrs. River mouths were easy to pinpoint. This was vital, as they could then establish their drift and the wind speed, before setting course for the next turning point inland. They usually approached the coast at about 8000 feet which was high enough for them to get a good wide view, to establish their position against the map, and also avoid any light flak in the area. Landfalls were also chosen to avoid heavy flak concentrations like those around Caen and Le Havre.

On this operation they flew east from Le Crotoy to Douai, and then turned towards the target, which was pin-pointed at 22.59 hrs. No lights were seen, so they circled the area three times at 700 feet. For a moment Jack saw a light, which went out immediately, and so they abandoned the operation and returned to Tempsford.

During the next moon period the Squadron lost its CO. Wing Commander Farley flew as a last-minute substitute in an otherwise mostly Polish crew on an operation to Czechoslovakia on 20/21 April. The Halifax crashed into a hill at Kreuth in Bavaria, killing all on board, including a number of agents who were about to be dropped.

Jack's next mission was on the night of 24/25 April, on an operation that had four code-names, *Lamb*, *Mule*, *Sable* and *Retriever*. Jack was again flying Whitley Z9282, and took off at 21.30 hrs. They made landfall at Le Crotoy at 22.25 hrs and then set course for a wood north of Valenciennes, which was reached at 00.14 hrs. After rivers, canals, or lakes, woods were the best ways to pin-point positions inland, especially large woods. Owen then turned on course for the drop zone, which should have been reached in 13 minutes. They could not pin-point their position and a search was made until 01.45 hrs, when the operation was abandoned. They brought back the containers, which were jettisoned over Tempsford, and a landing was made still carrying their 'passengers'.

Jack's third operation as captain was equally frustrating. Operation *Manfriday* on 27/28 April involved flying to Arras, again in the same Whitley, and then changing course for the drop zone. Despite a search for some time at only 1000 feet, no lights were seen. Once again he had to bring the containers home, landing at 03.50 hrs.

Finally, on the night of 29/30 April he had more success. He took off at 22.04 hrs on Operation *Luckyshot*, and crossed the French coast at 00.18 hrs, then setting course for the River Meuse. The target was found, and when the correct lights were lit they dropped the container and the pigeons they were carrying on target. Two men were seen to run to the container in the moonlight. They then set course for home, landing jubilantly at 05.10 hrs.

The successful drop was followed quickly by two more. On 1/2 May Jack flew Whitley Z9159 on Operation *Dastard*. His crew map-read their way at 2000 feet to La Ferté, and then set course for the target. Lights were seen immediately and a container dropped. They then flew to Beauvais where a consignment of pigeons was dropped. Then on the night of 24/25 May they performed a second drop under Operation *Luckyshot*, crossing the coast at Le Crotoy, and going via the River Meuse to the drop zone. The containers were dropped from 600 feet when the lights were spotted.

On the 29/30 May, a drop for Operation *Periwig* once more had to be abandoned shortly after take-off because of engine trouble. This was repeated the following night when Jack took off in Whitley Z9287 at 22.13 hrs on Operation *Mandamus*, but experienced engine trouble once more and landed back at Tempsford at 23.44 hrs.

During May the French SOE units had been destroyed by German Intelligence, and until September there were very few pick-ups or drops in France. Some of the Whitley crews went on normal bombing missions, to keep their hands in.

On 31 March Jack Owen was sent to Holland instead in an operation code-named *Catarrh*. Only a few days earlier, on the night of 27/28 March another Whitley, with Pilot Officer Widdup in command, had been lost on a supply drop for Operation *Catarrh*. Widdup had also dropped an agent code-named *Watercress*, but he was captured almost immediately. The Whitley had gone missing on its way back over the North Sea.

Jack flew Whitley Z9288, taking off at 22.45 hrs for the Zuider Zee. They had trouble finding the target in poor visibility, but did so eventually and the containers were dropped. Whether they actually reached the Dutch Resistance is open to question. A previous drop for Operation *Catarrh* by Pilot Officer Russell on 23 April, had also been delayed by lights that were difficult to see, having been placed in a wood. The containers eventually fell, straight into the hands of the Germans, who were waiting for them. The Germans had a flak battery sited to fire if the SOE realised the Dutch organisation had been compromised, and sent an aircraft to bomb the target. When only containers dropped from the sky the German AA guns remained silent so as not to give away the fact that they were there.

On the night of 3/4 May Jack's crew returned to France with a second attempt to drop supplies under the code-name Operation *Mandamus*. They crossed the coast at the mouth of the River Meuse at 00.20 hrs, but could not find the drop zone, and the mission was abandoned.

On the 25/26 June they flew straight to the drop zone in Whitley Z9202 for Operation *Spaniels*, and dropped their containers. Unfortunately, one of the containers failed to release and they had to bring it back.

The following night they had another drop under Operation *Luckyshot*, which was living up to its code-name. In an almost standard mission they took off at 22.40 hrs, crossed the coast at Le Crotoy at 00.23 hrs, flew to the River Meuse, ran in straight to the target and dropped the containers once the lights were seen. Once more, one of the containers hung up, and Jack turned the Whitley round for a second run. The reception committee seemed to have gone already, so they took the container back to Tempsford.

By June 1942 No. 138 Squadron had only four Whitleys ready for operations with another held in reserve. They were gradually being completely replaced by Halifaxes, and by June there were ten of these on charge with two more in reserve. Previously, the Halifaxes had only been used for long-range operations, but now their greater capacity was being exploited even on operations to northern France. Bomber Command had ceased using Whitleys completely by now, and the two Special Duties Squadrons would also soon give them up.

It was not for another month, on the night of 25/26 July that Jack, by now promoted to flight sergeant, and about to be promoted again to pilot officer, had another operation. It was to be his last. The Whitley used was once more to be his usual Z9282. His crew, which might have been his regular crew, though the Squadron's Operations Record Book, does not give details, included Sergeant D Thornton as second pilot. The observer was Sergeant J Whalley, the wireless-operator was Flight Sergeant WG Rock and the rear gunner was an Irishman, Sergeant PH Avery.

They took off from Tempsford for a drop zone in the Calvados region of north-west France. Landfall would probably have been between Coburg and Ouistreham, where the coastline formed a natural funnel, leading them

45. The graves of Jack Owen's crew in Vire cemetery, just after the War.

in, and they avoided the heavy anti-aircraft batteries at Le Havre and the lighter flak around Caen.

When they reached the area of the drop they could see no lights. Jack handed over control to Thornton and went back into the fuselage to try and see the ground better. As they circled at low altitude looking for the lights, Jack suddenly realised that they were much too low. He called over the intercom for Thornton to get the nose up, but it was too late. The Whitley crashed into high ground. Only Sergeant Avery in the rear turret survived the crash, and he was made a prisoner of war.

The other four crew members were buried in the local town cemetery at Vire, with simple wooden crosses. A number of Germans were buried in a line behind them. After the War the Germans were moved but Jack Owen and his crew remained where they were, in graves carefully looked after by the people of Vire, who they had come to help all those years before. The crosses were replaced by standard RAF gravestones, and Jack Owen's reads:

1166741 Flight Sergeant J Owen, Pilot, Royal Air Force
26th July 1942, Age 21

To a beautiful life came a sudden end, he died as he lived, everyone's friend

46. The graves as they are kept today.

CHAPTER 12

Down on the Dark Peaks

Even in the middle of summer there are wild and inhospitable places in England, where an aircraft can crash-land and the crew await rescue in vain, places where a crashed aircraft can lie undiscovered for weeks. This is the story of one such aircraft, and the crew who died of exposure while waiting for rescue.

The 338th production Boulton Paul Defiant was serial N3378. A standard Mark I, it was delivered to No. 19 MU, the Aircraft Storage Unit at St Athan, on 29 November 1940. On 8 December it was issued to No. 255 Squadron at Kirton in Lindsey in Lincolnshire.

No. 255 Squadron had only just been formed, on 23 November, at Kirton in Lindsey. It was one of two dedicated night-fighter squadrons to be equipped with Defiants formed that day, the other being No. 256 at Catterick. With the *Luftwaffe* beginning its night attacks, which were to become known as the Blitz, the Defiant was the best night-fighter available in any numbers, faster than the Blenheim and more effective than single-seaters. The two day-fighters squadrons, No. 141 and No. 264, and a new Polish squadron, No. 307, had all just been switched to night-time operations, and now No. 255 and No. 256 Squadrons joined them. During the winter two Hurricane night-fighter squadrons, No. 96 and No. 151, were also to receive Defiants.

No. 255 Squadron became operational on 5 January 1941, but did not fly its first patrols until the 9th, and did not have its first contact until 15 January when Flight Lieutenant RM Trousdale and Sergeant Chunn saw a Dornier Do 215. However, they did not get within range before it disappeared in the dark of the night. On the 10 February this same crew saw a Heinkel He 111 over the Humber and fired three bursts, claiming it as a probable, one of two claimed by the Squadron that night.

The Defiant usually flown by Trousdale and Chunn was N3378, but it was the squadron commander, Squadron Leader Roddick Lee Smith, and his gunner, Pilot Officer Eric Farnes, who were flying it on 5 May 1941 when it had its first victory. Taking off at 01.05 hrs they encountered a Junkers Ju 88, and shot it down seaward of Donna Nook. Smith was a regular officer, having joined the RAF on 15 March 1915. After a spell with No. 19 Squadron he had been transferred to the Fleet Air Arm, flying floatplanes at Calshot, and then Nimrods and Ospreys, both onshore and aboard HMS *Furious*. On 10 June 1940 he was posted to No. 151 Squadron as a Flight Commander flying Hurricanes.

He destroyed a Do 17 on 13 August and later claimed two more probables and two damaged. On 24 November 1940 he was posted to Kirton in Lindsey to command No. 255 Squadron.

His usual air gunner Eric Farnes was another Battle of Britain veteran. He had joined the RAF in 1940 and was posted to the second Defiant squadron, No. 141, at Turnhouse in July. The Squadron went south on 10 July and on 19 July they were ordered to cover a convoy off Dover. The nine Defiants that took off were bounced by thirty Bf 109s, and though four of the German fighters were shot down, so were six of the Defiants. Farnes' aircraft, L7001, was badly hit, and Farnes baled out. His pilot, Flight Lieutenant MJ Loudon, was severely wounded, but managed to crash-land the aircraft near Hawkinge. Farnes was rescued from the sea uninjured and later posted to No. 255 Squadron.

The usual pilot for N3378, Flight Lieutenant Richard Macklow Trousdale, was a New Zealander. He had applied for a Short Service Commission in February 1938 and sailed for England on 1 February 1939. On completion of his training he was posted to No. 266 Squadron flying Spitfires. Over Dunkirk he claimed a Bf 110 probable kill on 2 June, and in the Battle of Britain destroyed a Bf 109 on 16 August. He claimed a Bf 109 probable on 18 August, shared a Do 17 on 7 September and shot down another Bf 109 on 29 October. He had been posted to No. 255 Squadron as a flight commander on 23 November, and teamed up with Sergeant Chunn as his air gunner.

On 8 May, three days after Smith's success, Trousdale and Chunn were back on board N3378 when they saw a German bomber at 20,000 feet but were unable to catch it. The following night, No. 255 Squadron had its most successful night ever, shooting down six German bombers when a large force attacked Humberside. Trousdale and Chunn were again flying N3378 and shot down two of the Germans in 10 minutes. They shot down a Heinkel He 111 a few miles south-east of Leconfield at 01.40 hrs, and then at 01.50 hrs shot down another over the North Sea.

On 15 May the Squadron moved from Kirton in Lindsey to another Lincolnshire airfield at Hibaldstow, and from August began converting to Beaufighters. The Defiants still flew patrols for some weeks and N3378 was used by other aircrew. For instance, on 8 August Pilot Officer Ballantine and Sergeant Bayliss took off on a patrol at 23.20 hrs and were vectored after a raider, but were unable to find it. On 17 August Pilot Officer Clarke and Sergeant Allen flew on a patrol in N3378 over Flamborough Head. The following night Sergeant Turner and Sergeant Bedford flew a patrol in it from 22.50 hrs to 00.10 hrs.

Pilot Officer James Craig, a Scotsman, had joined the Squadron on its formation, his regular gunner being Bert Hill. His mechanic was another Scotsman, Bob Robertson, and his airframe rigger was John Hill. They flew their share of patrols over the winter of 1940/41 but were unable to make any contacts. Bob Robertson became worried about his wife, after he had not heard from her for a long time, during the period when Lancashire cities were being bombed. James Craig arranged to air-test his Defiant, and took Robertson in the turret, on what was to be his first flight.

The 'air-test' happened to take them over Lancashire and Craig landed at Burtonwood, which was only 20 minutes away from Robertson's house. At the far end of the runway, out of sight of the control tower, Robertson levered his 6 foot frame out of the turret, hopped down and ran for the perimeter fence. Craig returned to Lincolnshire without him. Robertson returned two days later, to face the charge of being absent without leave.

With the conversion to Beaufighters almost complete, the Squadron stood down on 23 August, and many of its members went on leave. Craig took N3378 to Scotland to visit his parents, and gave another lift, this time to Leading Aircraftman George Hempstead, another one of the Squadron's ground crew. They took off from Turnhouse on their return at 08.08 hrs on 29 August. About half an hour later, Craig contacted Kirton in Lindsey by radio and informed them that he was returning to base, presumably Hibaldstow, but he never arrived.

The following day the Squadron sent up nine Beaufighters and a Defiant to search along the route he should have taken, and the Army Co-operation Squadron at York also contributed two aircraft. After 32 hours of flying nothing was found. There were further searches on 31 August, but on 1 September the weather was too bad for flying. Finally, on the 2 September three aircraft returned to the search but again nothing was found.

47. James Craig (right) with his parents in Edinburgh.

It was not until 23 September that the crash site of N3378 was discovered, at Near Bleaklow Stones, in the Peak District, very near to the top of Bleaklow Moor. This was miles away from their logical route, which would have been down the east coast. David and Joe Shepherd, who had a farm in the Glossop area, came across the crash site, and the two men. They had survived the crash, and Craig had treated the more badly injured Hempstead. In the end, however, they had succumbed to their injuries and exposure, waiting for rescue.

Their bodies were taken down off the Moor to Glossop Police Station Mortuary, and Pilot Officer Craig was buried at Kirton in Lindsey on 26 September. The following day members of No. 10 Barrage Balloon Unit sent a message to No. 255 Squadron to say that they had visited the crash site and had found bullet holes in the wreckage, suggesting that this was due to enemy action.

The reason for the aircraft being considerably off course had never been discovered. The 'bullet' holes suggested enemy action, but there were no known German aircraft operating over the north of England that day. It was rumoured that a Spitfire from one of the units operating in the Teesside area had fired on the Defiant by mistake, but some of the 'bullet' holes were in the Defiant's radiator. It is hard to see how the aircraft could still have been flying over Derbyshire if it had lost all its coolant over Teesside, and even harder to see why Craig would not have tried to land immediately. No evidence to support this rumour has ever been found, the official inquiry stated simply that the aircraft hit high ground while flying in cloud.

A far more likely reason for the aircraft being off course was that James Craig's wife was living with her parents in Regent House, Belle Vue, Wakefield, just a few minutes' flying time from the crash site. Craig would not have been the first pilot to make a detour to fly over a loved one's house, and not the first to die as a result. The weather was generally good on 29 August 1941, but there was cloud lying on the Moors. The summit of Bleaklow Hill is 630 metres high, the crash site at Near Bleaklow Stones just north of the summit is at 600 metres.

Climbing away from the Yorkshire side of the Pennines in cloud, Craig hit the moor a glancing blow only 100 feet from the top, the greatest damage being to the port side of the aircraft. Defiant N3378 was not the only aircraft to find that cloud can become very solid indeed over the Dark Peak; over fifty crash sites litter the Moor. Craig and Hempstead, as they dragged their broken bodies from the wrecked aircraft, must have been shocked both by the suddenness of the crash, and the abrupt silence of the mist-shrouded Moor.

Even in August, Bleaklow Moor can be a cold and forbidding place, as I can testify myself. Even if Craig were capable of walking for help, he could easily have become lost in the mist and circled helplessly until collapsing. Staying with the aircraft was probably his best option, but the rescuers never came.

Much of the wreckage of N3378 remained on the Moor, but with the emergence of aviation archeology as a popular pastime in the 1960s and 1970s, parts of it were taken away by enthusiasts from all over the country. The fin was removed by a gentleman in nearby Hadfield who had a particular reason: he had made Defiant fins during the War at Northern Aircraft Ltd. The intact starboard tailplane and elevator were carried down by someone from Hyde in Cheshire and the last 8 feet of rear fuselage was carried down by a group from Macclesfield. They carried a wheel up the Moor with the intention of putting it in the surviving tailwheel fork and wheelbarrowing the fuselage down. But things were not as easy as that, and they ended up carrying it; with the extra weight of a tailwheel! The rear fuselage moved on to Kent and then to the Tangmere Aircraft Museum for a while, before ending up in Oxfordshire.

An RAF Halton party recovering the engines from a Blackburn Botha wreck a quarter of a mile away also took down parts of N3378: the turret ring, windscreen, propeller hub and one blade and a couple of small panels, including an inspection panel with the serial stencilled on. They went into the RAF Museum storage unit at Cardington for the next 20 years.

In 1993 the Boulton Paul Association, aware that there was only one

**48. Undercarriage leg and engine of Defiant N3378 on Bleaklow
Moor in 1996.**

surviving Defiant, N1671 in the RAF Museum, began collecting Defiant
parts to create a display of the aircraft in the town of its origin. Having
acquired the starboard tailplane and elevator, they quickly concentrated on
tracking down further parts of N3378, and all the above mentioned parts
were acquired over the next two years. In addition, they made the arduous
trek up to Near Bleaklow Stones on several occasions to bring down what
little remained, including parts of the starboard wing and the crushed and
broken port side of the tailplane. To this they added parts from other
Defiants, such as a turret cupola. In 1996 they were able to put on display
'Wolverhampton's own Defiant' in an exhibition of Boulton Paul's 60 years
in the town.

The search goes on for further parts of N3378 and any other Defiant. In
particular, they are seeking a section of wing from N3378, on which was at

least half a roundel. It was reported at the site in the late 1970s, but has since disappeared. The creation of the world's second complete Defiant seems unlikely, but as they already have far more of the aircraft than they ever thought possible, who knows!

All the parts of N3378 have been placed on display as a crash-site diorama, as a lasting memorial to the two men who died awaiting rescue on that lonely hillside in 1941, and of an aircraft that played its part in winning the War.

9. The re-creation of the crash-site of N3378 in the Boulton Paul Aircraft Heritage Project 2003.

CHAPTER 13

Pancake in the Black Country

The Black Country has never provided many places to land an aircraft. Before the Industrial Revolution it was an under-populated area of hills and forests; but with the discovery of coal, small industrial towns grew up, expanded, and eventually coalesced into one large conurbation in which finding a piece of greenery to make a forced landing is usually a matter of luck. In making a successful forced landing, it also helps of course if you are one of the most famous test pilots in the country, flying the aircraft with which you are most associated.

Alex Henshaw was born on 7 November 1912, and was educated at Stratford and Lincoln. He learned to fly with the Skegness and East Lincolnshire Flying Club, on a de Havilland Moth, taking his A Licence in April 1932. Later that year he acquired Moth G-AALN, and then the Comper Swift G-ACGL, which he flew in the 1933 King's Cup Air Race. He came eighth overall and won the Siddeley Trophy, his first victory in a glittering air racing career.

The following year he raced his Leopard Moth in the King's Cup, and the year after that his Miles M2T. It was the King's Cup Jubilee Race that year and the first day took the competitors north from Hatfield to Renfrew in Scotland, and then back south and across the sea to Belfast. It was quite unusual for Northern Ireland to be included in the route, which meant the second day began with the long crossing of the Irish Sea, to England, into Wales and then back to Hatfield.

Unfortunately, Henshaw was forced to ditch his newly purchased aircraft in the Irish Sea. His Miles M2T, G-ADNJ, Racing Number '24', was one of two specially built for the race. It was a single-seat low-wing monoplane based on the Miles Hawk, powered by a special 150 hp Cirrus Major R engine. He was skimming the waves only 10 feet up off Malin Head, when suddenly the engine stopped. His choices were singular. He stood up in his seat and stalled the aircraft when its flying speed had drained away. When the Miles hit the waves he was catapulted forward into the water.

The wooden monoplane remained intact and remained afloat, so Henshaw was able to swim back to it and climb aboard. Luckily, Jim Melrose in his Percival Gull saw the accident, and destroyed his own chances of winning the race by attracting the attention of the Isle of Man steamer to come and rescue his unfortunate rival. A boat was lowered and

Henshaw was rescued. His first forced/crash-landing had ended in almost immediate rescue.

On 30 December later that year Henshaw had another close call when he was forced to bale out of his Arrow Active, G-ABIX, over Lincolnshire, as it was on fire. In 1936 he flew his Leopard Moth to victory in the London to Isle of Man Race, but when he entered it in the King's Cup his race once more ended in a forced landing, when low oil pressure caused him to put down at Brockworth.

In 1937 he acquired the aircraft with which he will always be associated, apart from the Spitfire, Percival Mew Gull G-AEXF. He raced it in the 1937 King's Cup, but was unplaced, with a misfiring engine. For the 1938 race a new de Havilland Gipsy Six R engine was installed in the aircraft by Essex Aero, and Henshaw duly won the King's Cup at the record speed of 236 mph.

He then decided to make an attempt on the London to Cape Town record, and turned the aircraft back over to Essex Aero, to be prepared for the flight. Meanwhile, he and his father surveyed the West Coast route he intended to take, flying his new Percival Vega Gull, and making arrangements for fuel and oil to be ready at each of the airfields he planned to use. His meticulous preparations paid off and he broke the record with an astonishing time of 1 day 15 hours 25 minutes, and then returned in only 11 minutes more to break the return flight record as well. He still holds these records, to this day. The achievement brought him the award of the Britannia Trophy for the year 1938.

His achievements brought him to the attention of Jeffrey Quill, chief test pilot of Vickers Supermarine, who offered him a job testing the Spitfires that were beginning to roll off the production lines in ever increasing numbers. In June 1940 the first Spitfires were produced at the huge shadow factory built at Castle Bromwich, run initially by Austin Motors, but later taken over by Supermarine. Alex Henshaw went there as chief test pilot. During the War he personally flew 10 per cent of the 22,000 Spitfires built. The law of averages meant that some of those flights did not go according to plan.

On 18 July 1942 Henshaw flew a Spitfire Mk V, EP615, from Castle Bromwich to RAF Cosford, where there was a small Spitfire assembly plant based in some Bellman hangars on the edge of the airfield by the railway station. He had to test-fly another Spitfire Mk V, EP510, which had just been assembled at Cosford. As he came in to land at RAF Cosford he felt the starboard wing stall at 5 or 6 mph higher speed than it should have, and put this down to the camera door not being fastened and sealed properly. Unfortunately, he forgot to tell the mechanics to do this while he was testing EP510.

Thus, when he took off again in EP615 about an hour later the aircraft was in the same condition, not in itself dangerous, but to have serious consequences in a few minutes' time. There was complete cloud coverage at about 800 feet, and he decided to make the short 23-mile flight below the clouds. It was his last flight of the day and a few minutes later he was cruising over the edges of the Black Country, in the area of Willenhall, about halfway home.

Suddenly, without the slightest warning the Merlin engine stopped dead.

The cause was a skew-gear failure, which was a problem with the Merlin engine at the time. The skew-gear meshed with the magneto drive, and failure led to all ignition being instantly lost. Henshaw had already experienced such failures, the first being on another Spitfire he tested at Cosford, also at very low height. Being out in the country, Cosford was surrounded by suitable fields in which to make a forced landing. He chose a newly harrowed field and put the aircraft down in a satisfactory belly landing. This experience was followed by two more such failures which were both luckily within reach of Castle Bromwich and RAF Desford, so that he was able to make straightforward wheels down landings in both cases.

Over Willenhall he did not have such an easy decision. At such a low altitude the choice he had to make, to bale out or to try and put the aircraft down, had to be made almost instantly. He quickly decided to look for a place to force-land the Spitfire, and desperately scanned the soot-blackened landscape for a patch of greenery large enough.

There were factories and foundries packed around with streets of terraced houses and criss-crossed with power lines, canals and railways. Then he saw a stretch of greenery between two rows of houses. It was dotted with garden sheds and vegetable plots and there were a few trees on a patch of grass, but at the far end was a canal embankment, which he hoped would stop him if nothing else did.

As he turned his high speed glider, and lined it up, he had a few moments to consider his own mortality. He pulled the Sutton harness as tight as he could, and lowered the seat until he could hardly see out of the cockpit. Just before the Spitfire touched down the starboard wing stalled, and he suddenly remembered the open camera door. The aircraft swung to the right, and the starboard wing hit a large tree, which snapped it off at the root.

The remainder of the aircraft swung even more to the right and the propeller boss crashed into the kitchen wall of the end house. The propeller broke off and then the port wing dug into the earth, also snapping off. The fuselage crashed onwards, slowing up as it carved through the garden. The forward bulkhead hit something solid, which flung the fuselage up into the air, breaking it just behind the cockpit. Just before it turned over and buried Henshaw in a tangled mass of wreckage, it fell back with a final crash, and for the second time within a few minutes, a sudden silence descended.

Henshaw sat in the mangled wreckage for some time, his legs and thighs hurting badly. Blood was trickling down his hand and he suspected he had broken his arm. Blood was also trickling from his head and he closed his eyes to recover his senses, waiting for someone to cut him from the wreck. He could hear running water, but as he opened his eyes and his sense of smell took over, he realised with horror that it was actually petrol cascading over him, from the ruptured fuselage fuel tank.

Panic took over as the prospect of the wreck bursting into flames loomed large. He frantically undid his straps and pulled the canopy release lever. He scrambled hurriedly from the cockpit and was surprised to find himself standing shakily on his own two feet, apparently none the worse for wear apart from cuts and bruises. He heard weeping and shouting, and turned round to find an almost hysterical woman asking how many more poor souls

50. The tree that caught the starboard wing of Henshaw's Spitfire, and swung it into the house.

were in the wreck. He reassured her that it was a single-seater, and that he himself was not too badly hurt.

Just then a man came up, carrying that solution to all British problems in his shaking hands, a cup of tea. There was not much left in the cup by the time it reached Henshaw, but when he went to take a drink, he smelled the brandy with which it was laced, and had to decline, as he was a teetotaller. The man took the cup back, drank the tea himself, and set off to fetch another, unadulterated, cup. Henshaw discovered that he was near to Stubby Lane, Willenhall, and arranged to be picked up, arriving home to his wife somewhat later than he had expected.

In the nature of production testing, especially at a huge factory like Castle Bromwich, where thousands of aircraft were built, there were numerous forced landings; through the six years of the War, there were 127 in all, and these included Lancasters, Spitfires, Wellingtons and Seafires. Many of these were attributed to the Merlin's skew-gear, but that problem was eventually solved.

Of course, the test pilots at Castle Bromwich sometimes suffered the alternative nightmare to a sudden silence, that is a sudden loud bang, and sometimes the decision they had to make leaned towards leaving the aircraft to its own devices.

Later in the same year as his forced landing in Willenhall, Henshaw was testing another Mk V, MJ190, over Cannock Chase. There was a great deal of ground fog, and he had climbed through a cloud layer from 8000 to 17,000 feet. He was in a power-dive, writing on his knee-pad, when everything seemed to burst. A cloud of oil, glycol and smoke poured forth from the engine, which began vibrating very badly.

It was clear that even if he managed to slow the aircraft enough to stop it falling apart around him, the poor visibility conditions would leave him little if any time to find a suitable landing area. Getting out was the logical

51. The hole made by the Spitfire in the kitchen wall, and part of the fuselage.

option, and the knowledge that he was over the almost unpopulated area of Cannock Chase meant the aircraft was unlikely to crash onto any housing. Parts of the cowling were beginning to break away, but he still had time to scribble a note explaining his predicament on his knee-pad, in case he did not survive to bear witness to the problems.

He rapidly undid his straps, slid back the canopy and leaped from the cockpit. As he tumbled over and over he searched for the rip-cord, but even after finding it and feeling the sudden jerk as his canopy opened, his problems were not over. Looking up he could see that the parachute was damaged, and he had a long, agonisingly slow descent, with the further worry of having lost a boot. He finally landed in marshy ground, without damage to himself. After walking down a lane he came to a cottage where he phoned for a taxi to take him back to Castle Bromwich. Few of the episodes described in this book ended with such a simple return to civilisation for the pilots involved.

After the War Henshaw flew another Miles aircraft, a Messenger, out to South Africa. Here, he became a director of Miles Aircraft (Pty.) Ltd, but in 1948 returned to this country to run the family business.

52. The people of Willenhall had already paid for a Spitfire, so it was ironic that Alex Henshaw should return one to them, albeit in many pieces.

CHAPTER 14

Down in Greenland

During the Second World War, for the first time, aerial crossings of the North Atlantic became regular, daily events. Given the unpredictable, and unforgiving, weather conditions, it remained a hazardous venture. Over 500 aircrew lost their lives, most vanishing without trace. To ditch in the icy waters which the Ferry crews traversed was usually a death sentence. Even a forced landing on one of the land areas crossed on the northern route, over Greenland and Iceland, gave the crew little chance to survive. Nevertheless, the crew of an eastbound Douglas Boston did survive for fifteen days after a crash-landing on the Greenland ice cap.

The Atlantic Ferry Organisation (ATFERO) was initially a joint venture between Lord Beaverbrook's Ministry of Aircraft Production and Canadian Pacific Railways' Air Services Department. It was set up to fly North American-built aircraft to Great Britain, and eventually over 10,000 aircraft were flown over using several routes across the Atlantic. The scale of the operation was epic, especially when it is considered that before the War there had been only about 150 attempts to fly the Atlantic, a third of which had failed.

At first, the direct Gander to Great Britain route was flown by Hudsons with overload tanks in their bomb-bays, followed by Liberators and Catalinas, but for lighter twin-engined aircraft a new northern route was carved out. To supplement Gander a new starting airfield was created in the icy wilderness of Labrador at Goose Bay, and then staging airfields were built in Greenland and Iceland.

One of the types to be ferried extensively over this route was the Douglas Boston. One of these aircraft was BZ215, a Boston IIIA, one of 461 Bostons with BZ serials that were supplied to Great Britain under Lend Lease; though in the case of BZ215 'sent' to Britain would be a better description, as it was never to arrive.

On 10 November 1942 BZ215 left Gander for Iceland, with an all-RCAF crew. Its pilot was Pilot Officer David Goodlet, from Simcoe, Ontario; the navigator, in the nose of the aircraft, was Pilot Officer Alfred Nash from Winnipeg; and the radio operator was Flight Sergeant Arthur Weaver from Toronto. They took off at 0.800 hrs, heading for Bluie West One, an airfield built at the southern tip of Greenland at Narssarsuak. After a couple of hours they ran into fog, and heavy cloud cover prevented Nash from taking any sun shots. Then the radio failed, so they were unable to get bearings.

53. A Douglas Boston, from the same Lend-Lease batch of 461 aircraft with 'BZ' serials as Goodlet's Boston. The upper hatch is open, showing where the dinghy and vital radio gear were sited.

They flew at about 15,000 feet in case they drifted over the mountains of Greenland, hoping against hope that a break in the clouds would appear.

With fuel down to about half an hour's supply, Goodlet decided that they would have to try descending through the clouds while they still had engine power. They had no idea how low the cloud-base was or where they were. There was a serious danger that the cloud would stretch right down to the ground. They began descending cautiously through the cloud, not knowing whether they would simply crash into an ice-capped mountain at any moment.

They emerged from beneath the cloud at about 3800 feet and found themselves flying over a Greenland plateau between a range of mountains. They estimated that the coast was about 15 miles away, but they would have to climb back through the clouds to clear the mountains. That would mean making another blind descent, with no certainty that they would find anywhere more suitable to land. From the air the snow-covered ground beneath them looked flat enough, and they decided to try a wheels-up landing while they could. A wheels-down landing in a nosewheel aircraft was quite out of the question.

Anxious to make a landing while he still had some engine power to help him, Goodlet brought the Boston in for a landing straight away. He put it down on the three foot deep snow as gently as he could, and hoped to avoid any hidden crevasses. In the nose Alfred Nash felt horribly exposed, surrounded as he was by Perspex, and certain to arrive first at any obstacle to their plans.

As the Boston touched down Goodlet cut the switches, and the aircraft slid to a halt in a cloud of snow, largely in one piece. They were all able to exit the aircraft through upper hatches, from their three locations. Once they were certain that the aircraft was not going to burst into flames, they gathered together in the rear fuselage; surviving outside was out of the question. The weather was bitterly cold with the temperature around -40°F and a Force 8 gale blowing. They stuffed strips of parachute in the various cracks in the fuselage, and wrapped more of it them around themselves, but still the cold ate down to their bones.

They spent long periods lying on top of one another for the shared body heat, taking it in turns to be the one in the middle. At regular intervals they got up and kicked the skin of the aircraft to keep the circulation going in their feet.

Despite the cold, Weaver spent some time working on the radio transmitter. The radio racks were in the upper fuselage underneath a sideways folding hatch. He managed to get it going, and began transmitting an SOS. Ferry Command had assumed the aircraft lost when it became overdue, but two days later, on 12 May, Weaver's SOS was picked up. However, a search could not be made for several days because of the appalling weather conditions prevailing.

Goodlet and his crew had only a tin of rock-hard biscuits to sustain themselves; apart from the knowledge that their SOS had been acknowledged, and that they had not been totally abandoned. Realising that they could not be rescued from their present position, they made plans to drag their dinghy to the coast, from where they could paddle to the nearest settlement 100 miles away, if they were not picked up by a ship or flying boat.

On the sixth morning the weather had cleared enough for them to make the attempt. They destroyed the bomb-sight and burned all the aircraft's papers, as required in standing orders, though it is hard to see how any Germans would have come across them, lost in the wilderness of Greenland. They removed the life raft from its compartment behind the cockpit, and after inflating it, began dragging it across the snow.

Without any snowshoes they made only slow progress, struggling through the deep snow, and after two hours had only gone half a mile. Then it started snowing again. They took the sensible course of retreating to the aircraft where they survived the night as they had the previous five.

In the morning, the weather brought a welcome rise in temperature to about 54°F, and the snow turned to rain. They set off again for the coast, and that night was spent in soaking wet, freezing cold clothes, crouched under the dinghy for a little protection. The following day they continued their tortuous path, working their way around each crevasse in their way. They heard the engine of one of the searching aircraft and fired one of the flares from the dinghy.

Luckily, it was seen by the aircraft crew, who parachuted a bag containing food, clothing, sleeping bags, snowshoes, rope, and a very welcome bottle of scotch. It also contained instructions to rope themselves together, in case they fell down a crevasse, and to head in as straight a line for the coast as they could as a US Coastguard cutter was heading through the ice towards them.

After filling themselves with food and changing clothes, they spent a more comfortable night in the sleeping bags and then continued their arduous trek in the morning, made easier by the snowshoes. When they finally arrived at the coast they could see a ship about 10 miles out, and though they tried to light a fire to attract its attention they had nothing dry enough to burn. They spent that night helplessly watching the ship play its searchlights over the shore, without ever seeing them. In the morning a Catalina took off from near the ship and flew right over them without seeing them desperately waving their parkas.

That evening they watched in horror as the ship pulled up its anchor and started to sail away. After a dry day the wind had dried out their parkas, and in desperation they set light to them and got a good blaze going. Almost immediately the ship began firing flares and a Morse lamp began flickering. It told them to move back from the edge of the ice and to head south to meet a rescue boat.

They dragged themselves along the shoreline, working their way round obstacles until they came to a place where a boat could reach the shore. Six hours after they had been seen by the Coastguard cutter, *Northland*, they were finally picked up by one of its boats and taken on board, to its warm, welcome cabins. They had spent ten days in the icy Greenland wilderness, and against all the odds they had survived.

CHAPTER 15

Downed Lady

Occasionally, aircraft vanish without trace and then the wreckage is discovered many years later, usually with enough clues to reveal the reasons for the disappearance. Few such events have been quite so dramatic as the disappearance of a Consolidated B-24D Liberator named *Lady be Good*, and its rediscovery sixteen years later.

The name *Lady be Good*, from the George Gershwin song, was given to the B-24, serial 41-24301, at Morrison Air Force Base, Florida, when its new crew assembled in late March 1943, led by Flight Lieutenant William J Hatton of New York City. The second pilot, Second Lieutenant Robert Toner, came from North Attleboro, Massachusetts, but the rest of the crew came from a swathe across the states of the Mid-West.

Two, Second Lieutenant John Woravka and S.Sgt Vernon Moore came from Ohio, and two others, T.Sgt Harold Ripslinger and T.Sgt Robert Lamotte, came from Michigan. Second Lieutenant DP Hays came from Lee's Summit, Missouri, S.Sgt Guy Shelley from New Cumberland, Pennsylvania, and S.Sgt Samuel Adams from Eureka, Illinois.

Lady be Good was a standard B-24D model with Pratt & Whitney R-1830-43 engines. It had twin 0.5-inch guns in dorsal and tail turrets, single 0.5-inch waist guns on each side, a 0.5-inch tunnel gun and two 0.5-inch guns in hand-held mountings on each side of the glazed nose.

The crew were assigned overseas duty almost straight away and left for North Africa to join the 376th Bomb Group, 'The Liberandos', based at Solluch near the eastern shore of the Gulf of Sirte, on the narrow Libyan coastal strip south of Benghazi. The 376th Bomb Group had been activated at Lydda in Palestine on 31 October 1942 and began bombing raids almost immediately. They were later to become famous for the low-level raid on the Ploeşti oil fields in 1943, but for the first part of the year, together with the 98th Bomb Group they were engaged in operations against Italy.

They had moved to Abu Sueir in Egypt, then Gambut in Libya, and Solluch on 22 February, where Colonel Keith Compton became the new CO, replacing Colonel George McGuire. Hatton and his crew were assigned to the 514th Bomb Squadron, within the group.

On 4 April Hatton and his crew were briefed on their first mission, along with the crews of twenty-four other B-24s of the 376th. Take-off was planned for 13.30 hrs, timed to hit some of the airfields around Naples at twilight. If all went to plan they would complete the 1500-mile round trip by around midnight.

The Liberators were having trouble with sand in the Pratt & Whitney R-1830 engines, and several experienced such trouble on the long flight over the Mediterranean. Nevertheless, eleven crews claimed to have bombed the primary target, with the others bombing the secondary. Four aircraft of the second section, including *Lady be Good*, found cloud cover obscuring the target, and turned back while still 30 miles away.

One of these four landed on Malta, short of fuel, and two more landed back at Solluch, together with the rest of the force. The only aircraft that had not returned by midnight was *Lady be Good*.

There was a heavy overcast over the whole of the North African coastline, and the rookie crew were fearful that their navigation had gone awry and that they were too far to the west. At 00.10 hrs they called Benina for a radio fix. The tower gave them a fix estimating them at 330 degrees, to the north-west, which was on the direct route from Naples. The fix was acknowledged by Hatton. That was the last contact anyone had with *Lady be Good*. Having apparently disappeared without trace, it was assumed that the Liberator had run out of fuel and had gone down in the sea. Despite air searches, nothing was found. The nine crew members were posted Missing in Action.

'The Liberandos' began the move from Solluch to Benghazi only two days later, later in the year moving to Tunisia, and then on to Italy. *Lady be Good* was a forgotten mystery.

It was not for sixteen years that the final fate of *Lady be Good* was discovered. In November 1958 an aircraft operating with an oil prospecting team spotted the wreck and marked it on their maps. It was 440 miles inland in an area of flat, barren, sun-scorched desert. From the air it looked like a recent wreck. The B-24 lay on its belly with its fuselage broken around the site of the hatch guns, for all the world as if the crew had just made a belly landing; but no Liberator had operated in the area for many years. A C-47 was dispatched from Wheelus Air Force Base, with a doctor on board, and landed alongside on the flat, gravelly surface.

The hundred yard walk from the C-47 to the wreck, in the absolute silence of the desert, and heat in excess of 50°C in the shade, was an apprehensive one. They did not know what they would find, though they expected the grisly remains of the Liberator's crew.

Around the bomber was a scattering of debris, sheepskin flying clothes, oxygen bottles, flak helmets, and first aid kits; which seemed to show that someone had got out of the wreck. The metalwork was bright and shiny with no sign of corrosion anywhere. The aircraft number '64' and the name *Lady be Good* being noted on the forward fuselage.

Inside the fuselage, flying clothes hung limply on hooks, and vacuum flasks still contained warm drinkable coffee! The radio was still working, which came in handy for the C-47 crew whose own radio was unserviceable. The guns were still in the dorsal and tail turrets and in the nose, but there were no parachutes inside the aircraft, which was the first clue to what had happened.

It was found that three of the engines were out of fuel and the propellers feathered. The automatic pilot was set and the aircraft trimmed for a high rate of descent even with the last engine running. The C-47 returned to

54. The Consolidated Liberator *Lady be Good* as it was found in 1958.

Wheelus and an investigation into what had happened to *Lady be Good* was set in motion.

The early history of the crew and the official version of what had happened on their first mission was traced through official records. It was obvious that when Hatton had radioed Benina for a fix, thinking he was still over the Mediterranean, he had actually already overflown the base and was

55. *Lady be Good*, and in the background, the C-47 that flew in from Wheelus Air Force Base to examine the wreck.

well to the south-east. The direction-finding equipment of the time could not distinguish between opposite headings. A bearing of 150 degrees (the actual direction of the B-24) would seem the same as 330 degrees, and the classic 180-degree error was made.

As Hatton and his crew flew on looking for signs of the coast, they were actually getting further and further inland. As the aircraft began running out of fuel, Hatton ordered the crew to bale out while he trimmed the aircraft to fly level on the one remaining engine. Attempting to make a forced landing in the darkness would have been a risky venture, especially as there was high ground near the Libyan coast, extending up to over 2500 feet. In any case, wheels-up landings in high wing aircraft are always dangerous. In the Liberator the fuselage tended to crumple up. It must have been something of a shock to the crew to come down on dry land, instead of in the sea. The aircraft flew on to make a passable crash-landing all by itself.

A party equipped for a land search, including Hiller 12 helicopters, was sent out from Wheelus. They discovered signs that some of the crew had come down in a slight depression about 8 miles from the wreck. Three flight boots were arranged in the shape of an arrow. It seemed probable that the crew made their way to the B-24 to equip themselves to walk out of the desert. They probably signalled their whereabouts to one another with their side-arms, and an empty .45 calibre clip was found about 12 miles from the wreck.

They must have thought they were not far from the sea, which they reasoned must lie to the north. The search party followed a trail of clothing and other items, some of them obviously left deliberately, including cut-up pieces of parachute harness and stones, marking their route to the north. They walked at night, sheltering from the blistering heat during the day in the shade of their parachutes. The realisation of their tragic navigational error must have dawned slowly upon them, and their mental calculations of the time spent in the air and therefore the distance travelled since receiving the bearing from Benina, will have weighed heavily on their sweating shoulders.

The trail they left finally ended on the edge of the Sea of Calanscio, an area of huge sand dunes. It is possible the nine exhausted men thought they were at last at the edge of the sea, but as they struggled up the shifting sand of each massive dune, only a vista of more and more sand spread before them.

After four months the search was abandoned, but in February 1960, oil prospectors found five bodies on the up slope of a sand dune, and one, Second Lieutenant Robert Toner, had kept a diary. He related how eight of the crew had joined up, and on the morning of Monday, 5 April had set out for the north. They struggled on through the heat of the day, probably still certain they were near the sea. That night the desert, as usual, became bone-numbingly cold, and they huddled in their parachutes, but could not get warm, so they decided to continue their trek. They walked on until 11.30 the following morning, and then rested through the heat of the day. They rationed themselves to a cup of water each per day per man, but by Wednesday morning the water was already half gone.

By Friday, after travelling over 70 miles, they reached the sea of sand, and only three could continue, Vernon Moore, Guy Shelley and Harold 'Rip' Ripslinger. The five remaining huddled together praying for a search plane, hoping their companions would bring help, but none came. Toner's diary told of their terrible pain, and his last entry was on Monday 11 April, after one week in the desert. It read 'No help yet. Very cold nite'.

The oil prospectors searched for the other three men but found nothing, three months later they came across the body of Harold Ripslinger 20 miles to the north, and then that of Guy Shelley 7 miles further on. As each had dropped, his companion had struggled on. Vernon Moore was never found.

The sands of the Libyan Desert have hidden many things over the centuries, including the final resting place of the soldiers of many nations. For sixteen years they hid the fate of nine young Americans, the crew of the *Lady be Good*. One of the propellers from *Lady be Good* was used in a memorial erected at Wheelus Air Force Base, and later moved to the United States Air Force Museum at Wright-Patterson Air Force Base, Dayton, Ohio, when Wheelus closed. The accompanying plaque read:

> The Propeller is from the four-engined
> B-24 Liberator bomber serial Number 41-24301
> *'LADY BE GOOD'*
> which crashed in the Libyan desert 880 miles
> Southeast of Wheelus Air Force Base on 5th April 1943
> after a bombing raid on Naples, Italy. The aircraft
> operating from an airfield near Benghazi with the 514th
> Bomb Squadron was reported missing
> in action and its fate was not known
> until discovery of the wreckage in
> May 1959. Subsequent searches in the Libyan
> desert recovered remains of eight of
> her nine crew members
> Placed 19th January 1961.

Also displayed at Wright-Patterson is a machine gun from *Lady be Good* together with the navigator's charts, compass and canteen. Also on display is a stained glass chapel window, which was paid for by the people at Wheelus Air Force Base to commemorate the crew of *Lady be Good*. It was also brought to Wright-Patterson when Wheelus closed.

CHAPTER 16

Down in the Arctic Ocean

Ditching an aircraft in the iceberg-strewn, Arctic waters of the North Atlantic is not recommended, and seeking refuge on one of the barren islands of rock in those icy seas hardly increases your chances of rescue. Yet one Ferry Command crew ferrying an aircraft, unusually in a westward direction, had just such an experience.

In the middle of 1943 the North Atlantic ferrying operation of ATFERO was taken over by the RAF's new Transport Command, and the operation over the North Atlantic became the province of No. 45 Group of Ferry Command. Most of the aerial traffic was west to east, with the Liberators of the Return Ferry Service bringing the pilots back the other way. However, a few aircraft were ferried in the opposite direction, including twenty-two war-weary Handley Page Hampdens, only one of which failed to complete the journey.

Captain Robert E Coffman from Louisiana, Flying Officer Norman E Greenaway from Alberta and their wireless operator Ronald E Snow from Nova Scotia were an RCAF crew assigned to No. 45 Group, normally ferrying aircraft east, and then returning by transport aircraft to Canada. In late October 1943 they found themselves with the job of flying themselves back to Canada in one of twenty-five Handley Page Hampdens, which were destined for No. 32 Operational Training Unit (OTU) at Patricia Bay near Vancouver. In the event, only twenty-two set off, the other three being too clapped-out even to attempt the journey

The Hampden they had drawn was AE309, one of 770 Hampdens built by English Electric in Preston. Delivered early in 1941, it served operationally with No. 144 Squadron, flying from Hemswell and then North Luffenham. It was then one of 144 Hampdens converted to torpedo-bombers. It did not return to No. 144 Squadron, which was one of two No. 5 Group bomber squadrons transferred to Coastal Command to operate Hampden torpedo-bombers, shortly afterwards being sent to Murmansk. Hampden AE309 remained in Britain and served with No. 5 OTU.

The chance to fly an aircraft back themselves, even a war-weary veteran like the Hampden, was not completely unwelcome. The usual way back was a very uncomfortable journey in a Liberator, in which the passenger accommodation was sitting on the planked-over bomb-bay wrapped under several layers of clothes to protect against the freezing cold weather, and possibly sucking on an oxygen tube if the captain was forced to fly at any altitude. The temperature in the bomb-bay could fall to as much as -40°F, and cases of frostbite were not unknown. Against the prevailing wind, and with the uncertain weather reporting which existed, the return journey was far from safe. Several Return Ferry Service Liberators were lost, together with their precious cargo of aircrew.

The flight in the Hampden, with its much shorter range, had to be by the Northern Route with relatively short stages, starting from Prestwick and going via Iceland, Greenland, and then on to Goose Bay in Labrador. The Hampden was unusual in having only room for one pilot, in a fighter-type cockpit and so Greenaway was accommodated in the navigator's position in the nose of the aircraft, with Coffman doing the flying. They had no trouble as far as Iceland, but two hours out of Iceland, flying at 9000 feet, the starboard engine stopped. They set course directly for Greenland where they hoped to crash-land, but the port engine was also giving trouble, though the old Hampden had little single-engined performance anyway. It had a tendency to go into a spiral dive when on one engine, and did so about an hour later when they were down to 4500 feet and Greenland was still 100 miles away. Coffman managed to restore level flight with a masterful piece of airmanship, but they lost a lot more altitude.

He nursed the faltering Pegasus engine for another 20 minutes as they struggled forward, bouncing around in a Force 8 gale. Although Snow was sending an SOS, reception was impossible as they were out of range of all ground stations.

Then, when they estimated they were still about 15 miles from Greenland, the port engine stopped. They were at less than 1000 feet, and as Coffman glided the stricken aircraft towards the stormy sea, they could see icebergs all around. A huge one, towering 100 feet out of the sea, loomed ahead. Coffman steered for the calmer sea in the lee of this behemoth. As his two companions braced themselves Coffman ditched the aircraft successfully, without the shattering crash they were expecting. The aircraft's dinghy was stored in the port engine nacelle, and was released automatically when the aircraft struck the water. This was a very welcome feature of the Hampden, which meant the crew did not have to man-handle it out of the fuselage as on most other aircraft; this probably saved their lives. The three of them grabbed the emergency kit and struggled out onto the wing, with the gale lashing round them and the icy sea breaking all around.

The dinghy was inflated and bobbing about alongside the wing. They were able to step into it, though they were already soaked through, and cut the cord securing it to the aircraft. Within 70 seconds of hitting the sea, the Hampden lifted its tail and slid beneath the waves. All they could do was to begin paddling west in the direction of Greenland, hoping they would not be run down by the icebergs that towered all around them. As darkness fell, they could still hear the bergs colliding and crashing, cracking like the sound of heavy artillery.

Frozen stiff, cold and wet, they paddled on, as much to keep up their body heat as anything, but certain they would have to reach the coast to survive. When they became overdue an air search would have been put into motion, but they were only a tiny dinghy in a huge ocean.

As dawn broke they were only a mile from the coastline. Able to see their destination, they paddled on, but as they neared the shore the coastal eddies tossed the dinghy back and forth. Rising from the sea just off shore was a

56. Hampden aircrew examine their dinghy, which was housed in the wing. Captain Coffman and his crew owed their lives to it.

huge 3000 feet, black rock, named Umanarsuk. It seemed to offer a safer and more immediate haven and they paddled into a sheltered cove.

They clambered onto a slippery shelf of rock and dragged their dinghy out of the water. They could see across the narrow stretch of water, only 50 yards wide, to the mainland, but it seemed far too dangerous to cross, and too cold to swim. They decided to wait for rescue where they were, and clambered up to a ledge about 100 feet above the sea, dragging their dinghy and deflating it to provide them with some shelter.

Within two hours of huddling together on their narrow ledge the three men heard the sound of aircraft overhead. The headquarters of the Atlantic Ferry Unit in Montreal had ordered an air search once the Hampden was known to be overdue and search planes were sent out from Iceland, Goose Bay and Newfoundland. The three men fired Very lights every time they heard engines, but there was a storm of sleet and snow immersing them in a cold grey blanket and the aircraft had to fly at altitude to avoid the Greenland ice cap.

They had twenty-seven cartridges with their Very pistol. In the emergency kit were forty-five malted milk tablets, twelve sealed pints of water, four squares of barley sugar, some chewing gum, some Benzedrine (amphetamine) tablets, a first aid kit, a yellow distress flag and a mirror, which could be used as a heliograph. In addition, each of them had some chocolate in their pockets, though this had been soaked in sea water.

They erected the distress flag, though not hopeful that anyone would see it, as their location was only visible from one direction. They planned a ration of the supplies, which would last seven days. Each was apportioned two malted milk tablets and a third of a pint of water per day, together with a small piece of chocolate. After four days huddled on their freezing slab of rock they began to despair of rescue, and halved the ration, though there was no shortage of water as they could eat snow, the only comfort that their perilous refuge afforded them.

The weather, already bad, became worse, and the storm force winds blew away their distress flag. The seas were so rough that the waves drenched their tiny ledge, even though it was 100 feet above the sea. They struggled higher up the barren rock and found an even narrower ledge about 250 feet above the crashing waves. For three days the storm raged, and the wild seas smashed against Umanarsuk and icebergs crashed into it.

After nine days of cold, desperate waiting, their spirits began to ebb, and they cut their ration even further to half a malted milk tablet a day. How they had survived so long in wet, freezing clothes as Arctic storms whipped around them is a testament to human endurance. On the morning of the ninth day they saw a small ship about 15 miles off shore. They took Benzedrine tablets that they had been saving for such an occasion, and fired six Very lights. The sky was overcast so they could not use the mirror to signal. After half an hour the ship turned away and left, and they subsided in disappointment.

That night a storm of snow and sleet hit the rock, and with their rations gone they faced up to an imminent death. In the morning they were too cold even to sit up, but when they heard the drone of an aircraft at low altitude, Coffman swallowed another Benzedrine tablet and fired one of the few remaining Very lights. But the aircraft climbed and flew away.

On the tenth night they struggled to keep one another awake, believing that to fall asleep would mean certain death. They lay frozen in their makeshift tent as dawn crept over them. They were all desperately thirsty and Snow offered to creep out and fetch some snow for them to eat. Shortly afterwards, he crawled back to inform them the unbelievable news that there was a stationary ship about 8 miles away.

They all crawled outside, and sure enough there was a small two-masted ship, heaved to offshore. Just at that moment the sun shone from behind the grey clouds. They began flashing with the heliograph mirror, but for three hours there was no response from the ship.

The ship was Norwegian, *The Polar Bjorn*, carrying some American Army officers to Greenland. They had heaved to with engine trouble while they made repairs. One of the American officers, Major John Crowell, came up on deck for a breath of fresh air. Crowell was an experienced man in Northern climes. He had been in charge of establishing and operating one of three weather stations, Crystal One, Two and Three, built by the Americans in Canada's Arctic North East. He had been landed on an island in Frobisher Bay and had built Crystal Two, together with a small airstrip and operated it through the previous winter. Crowell had been chosen for the job because he had been the mate on a schooner exploring Frobisher Bay a few years before.

On the deck of *The Polar Bjorn* Crowell saw a gleam from the barren rock to the east, but thought it nothing more than the sun catching on a piece of ice or snow. Then he thought he saw a puff of smoke followed by a glint of light that arched down into the sea. What he had seen was the very last Very light cartridge being used up by the three survivors.

Crowell fetched his binoculars and alerted the Norwegian captain. They realised that someone was signalling with a mirror, but thought for a while that it might be part of a U-Boat crew luring them into a trap. A boat was lowered but a well armed party was sent ashore, in case the signals were being made by Germans. All they found were the three frozen airman, who all passed out before they could be brought to the warmth of the ship, which soon set sail for port. Within hours they were safely in a Greenland hospital, three very lucky men indeed.

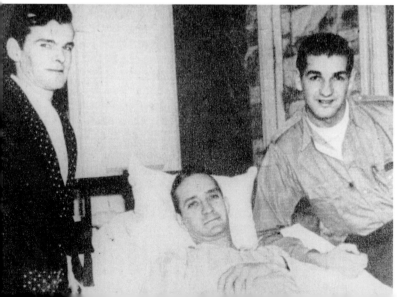

57. The Hampden's crew recovering in a Greenland hospital. Left to right: Robert Coffman, Norman Greenaway and Ronald Snow.

CHAPTER 17

A Dip in the Med

Flying down to Cannes in the south of France for a spot of sailing on the Mediterranean, has long been considered a very desirable way to pass the time. To have the flight paid for, and the boat supplied free of charge, would therefore seem to be a very attractive proposition. However, not if you are the crew of a Halifax bomber, hoping to make an immediate return flight to England, without landing.

Beginning life as a First World War squadron, and one of the many casualties of the resulting peace, No. 35 Squadron, re-formed at Bircham Newton on 5 November 1940 as the very first Handley Page Halifax squadron, and flew its first operation with the new aircraft on 10 March 1941. It began receiving Halifax IIs in January 1942, and moved to RAF Graveley in Huntingdonshire in August 1942 as part of the newly formed Pathfinder Force. It began to receive the Bristol Hercules-powered Halifax III in October 1943, but did not fly any operations with it until December.

On 11 November 1943, Pilot Officer JR Petrie-Andrews' crew were briefed as part of the Pathfinder Force on an operation against the railway marshalling yards at La Bocca, west of Cannes. These yards were on the main line between France and Italy. The task was to visually mark the target with green flares, which were to be dropped from not more than 10,000 feet. Despite the low height at which they were to operate over the target, they thought the sortie would be a piece of cake, a welcome relief from operations against the Ruhr, and Berlin. The total force operating would be 124 Halifaxes and 10 Lancasters, drawn from Nos 4, 6 and 8 Groups.

The south of France was considered a soft option compared with operations against Germany, but they were told that if they did get into trouble they could make for the island of Sardinia. Sardinia had just been occupied by the Allies following the Italian capitulation, but none of them thought, as they climbed aboard their Halifax, that this would be a haven they would need.

Petrie-Andrews' crew were very experienced, having completed seven operations with No. 4 Group, before being transferred to the Pathfinder Force with which they had completed another thirty-one. This would actually be their first operation since the night of 22/23 October, when they had been to Kassel in Germany. They had been briefed three times for operations against Germany in November, on 3rd, 7th and 9th, but they had all been cancelled before take-off.

Their aircraft was still one of the Merlin-engined Halifax IIs, HR929, coded TL-E, which had been built by Handley Page at Cricklewood and was actually an ex-405 Squadron aircraft. The navigator, Flight Lieutenant Jack Armitage and the bomb-aimer, Pilot Officer R Backhouse were sited in the cleaned up all-glazed nose, without the gun turret of earlier marks. The rear gunner, Flight Sergeant NW Barnett, had four 0.303 inch machine-guns in his Boulton Paul Type E turret, and the mid-upper gunner, WOG Dale, also had four .303s in his Boulton Paul Type A Mk III upper turret, a version of the famous Defiant turret. The wireless operator was Flight Sergeant HRM Stroud, and the seventh member of the crew was the flight engineer, Pilot Officer JH Morgan.

They took off from Graveley at 18.31 hrs, and their route took them almost due south and over the French Alps. Until they neared the target area, they were untroubled by anti-aircraft fire or night fighters. After crossing the Alps, the starboard outer engine began to give trouble and then gave up the ghost completely. This was the seventh time they had lost one of their engines on operations, so they were neither surprised nor alarmed. Completing the flight on only three engines was not a problem.

They made their run over the marshalling yards at only 3000 feet, a very low height chosen to make sure they marked the target accurately, but placing them at risk of drawing fire from even the lightest anti-aircraft guns. Just after Backhouse called 'Flares away' from his seated bomb-aiming position in the nose, there was a burst of light anti-aircraft fire. They were hit in the port inner engine, which was immediately put out of action.

With two propellers feathered they were in serious trouble, without enough power to get them back over the mountains. The haven offered to them by the island of Sardinia, suddenly looked a timely blessing. They signalled their situation and their intentions to base, and Fight Lieutenant Armitage began working out a course for Sardinia.

They decided to fly on a southerly course until they reached the right latitude and then turn east. They felt this provided a better chance of making a safe landfall, avoiding Corsica. They did not want to miss Sardinia, relatively large though it was, and fly on blindly across the Mediterranean until they ran out of fuel.

They had just made their turn to the east, at a point Armitage estimated to be about 50 miles west of Sardinia, when one of the surviving engines coughed, spluttered and just faded away. Slowly, on the power of the remaining Merlin, the Halifax lost height. Eventually, Petrie-Andrews called them to take ditching stations, and as the aircraft made its last dive towards the sea, Armitage checked the time. It was still only 22.40 hrs. With most of the crew safely behind the main spar, facing aft, they were ready to ditch.

Petrie-Andrews levelled out and pulled off a masterly forced landing on the surface of the sea, touching down at about 100 knots. The aircraft shuddered from nose to tail as it hit the sea, but did not disintegrate. The glazed nose caved in and water rushed through the fuselage, sending Armitage swirling round as if he were in a whirlpool. Once the aircraft came to a halt, and the first rush of water was over, the Halifax was left floating on the sea, but filling quickly with water.

58. A Halifax in the sea just after ditching, but not that of Petrie-Andrews, who did not have the security of another aircraft overhead to record his plight.

The crew stumbled and fought their way to the escape hatch, bumping into all the debris that was floating around in the fuselage. The flight engineer, Morgan, was frantically hitting the dinghy release button, but nothing was happening. Armitage struggled up to him and they both tried to pull the manual release lever, but without success. Afraid that the Halifax might sink at any moment, taking them with it, Morgan grabbed an axe and they made their way to the escape hatch and out onto the port wing. The rest of the crew gathered here as he used the axe to smash the wing panel, which covered the dinghy.

When he smashed the panel off they pulled the dinghy out, inflated it, and tossed it into the sea. As they were climbing in Petrie-Andrews realised there were only six of them, and that Backhouse was missing. He struggled back into the fuselage with Armitage, looking for the missing bomb-aimer. Inside the fuselage there was a strong smell of petrol. The Halifax had a large extra fuel tank in the bomb-bay and that must have ruptured. They found Backhouse floating in the water, amidst all the debris. The water was up to their waists as they pulled Backhouse to the escape hatch and out onto the wing.

They lowered him into the dinghy, and followed him down, casting off the mooring rope. Just at that moment the stricken Halifax performed a slow roll, luckily away from them, and sank beneath the waves. They applied artificial respiration to Backhouse who eventually began to show signs of life. When he came to, he explained that he had been out on the wing with them, but had decided to go back in and get the individual 'K' Type dinghies, in case they could not free the crew dinghy. Inside, he had been overcome by the 100 octane fumes, and had passed out.

Within a few minutes of being in the dinghy, most of the crew were sick, not because of the movement of the waves, the sea was quite calm, but probably because of a combination of the petrol they had swallowed and shock. Feeling much better after this, they began to examine the dinghy to find out what supplies there were.

There was no food at all, though someone produced an apple from their pocket, and there were not many tins of water. There was a dinghy radio and a supply of Very lights. Stroud, the wireless operator, began to rig the wireless but discovered that it was damaged, and beyond help. Petrie-Andrews noticed that the wind was blowing from the west, and so he took his parachute and made a sail with it, using two radio poles as masts, which had to be held upright manually. Taking it in turns to hold the poles in the brisk wind, they seemed to be making around 2 knots through the water, with every hope of eventually reaching the coast of Sardinia.

None of them were able to sleep that night, and when morning came, with it came a weather front sweeping in from the west. This tossed the dinghy about on a freshening sea, and very soon it was impossible to hold their makeshift masts aloft. They were soon crouching under the dinghy's canopy, seeking what meagre shelter it provided as they were tossed around on the ever-increasing seas.

All through 12 November they were tossed around on the sea, no one managing to get any sleep. That night some of them fell into a brief sleep, totally exhausted, but during the night were rudely awoken when the dinghy overturned. After much desperate effort the seven of them, working together with a great deal of shouting in the wind and darkness, managed to turn the dinghy the right way up, and hauled themselves back aboard.

Dawn on 13 November brought sudden new hope, as they could see the lighthouse on Asinara Island away to the right. Asinara lay just off Cape Falcone, the north-west corner of Sardinia. They manoeuvred the dinghy towards the island with the canvas paddles, but the closest they could get was about a mile. Petrie-Andrews wanted to dive in and swim to the lighthouse, but the sea was still rough and the others persuaded him not to try. The dinghy slid by the island still on course for Sardinia, but the visibility slowly worsened.

Nevertheless, at about 2 pm they sighted a cruiser going in the opposite direction, and their hopes soared once more. They fired off several Very lights, but the warship never saw them and sailed away, leaving them disappointed and depressed. There were only six tins of drinking water left, and the grim prospect of not being rescued for some time, led them to severely ration the remainder.

The wind dropped in the evening, which allowed them to re-erect the sail.

There was a strong swell but the night passed uneventfully. The monotony continued through 14 November, and they only had a few sips of water. They were grateful that it was November, and the full heat of the Mediterranean summer was not beating down on them. Just after 4 pm that day someone suddenly shouted 'There's land !' There, in clear view, was the northern tip of Sardinia.

There was great excitement as the wind and current was carrying them towards the land, but then the direction of the current changed and they found themselves being carried away from the island. They paddled for all they were worth, with the canvas paddles, but despite all their efforts did not seem to make much headway. They continued to paddle until after darkness fell, and then fired off Very lights at regular intervals. By 11 pm the shore was only a couple of hundred yards away, illuminated by the flares each time they were fired.

They made one last frantic effort, using what little energy they had left, and succeeded in beaching the dinghy on a flat rock at the base of some cliffs. As they sprawled on the rock recovering their energy, they heard voices on the cliffs above them, and then saw torches being carried down by a number of people. A group of Italians descended the cliffs and helped the exhausted crew to climb up to the lighthouse at Cape Testa, the extreme northern tip of Sardinia. They were welcomed wholeheartedly by the locals, who offered them a meal of spaghetti and coffee, and gave them a bed for the night.

In the morning the seven of them travelled to the Royal Navy headquarters at Maddelena, where they were put aboard a minesweeper *en route* to Ajjacio in Corsica. There, they were taken to the airfield and boarded a Dakota, which would take them back south again to North Africa. As they were waiting to take off, a Bf 109 appeared from nowhere and shot up the airfield, luckily without hitting the Dakota. From North Africa they were taken back to Great Britain in a Lancaster bomber.

Once home, they discovered that four other Halifaxes were lost on the same operation to Cannes, all shot down by German night fighters in the area of Calvados in northern France. Two of them were from No. 35 Squadron, HR798 and HR985, one from No. 78 Squadron, LW321, and one from No. 158 squadron, HR791. No. 35 Squadron's 'Milk Run' to the Mediterrean had thus resulted in the loss of three of their aircraft, one of their worst nights of the year. Their worst night ever had been the night of 21–22 June 1943, when they had lost six aircraft on an operation to Krefeld, the worse losses recorded by any squadron in 1943.

Yet, the La Bocca marshalling yards were not hit in the raid. Despite the low altitude at which the Pathfinders dropped their target markers, the railway yards were not hit by a single bomb. Most of them fell on the local suburbs of La Bocca, where thirty-nine French civilians died, and on the nearby village of Agay. Petrie-Andrews' crew's dip in the Mediterranean had been for nothing.

CHAPTER 18

Down on the Tundra

The very north of Scandinavia can be an inhospitable place, even when the midnight sun is shining round the clock, let alone as winter approaches. It is not a good place for an aircraft to force-land. It is barely populated and with good reason. Even finding a place to successfully force-land is not easy in a land of trees, lakes and mountains. There are few grassy fields and even fewer airfields, so it would be a lucky Lancaster crew who found a place to land in Lapland with their wheels down.

The Dambuster Squadron's second most famous target was the German battleship, *Tirpitz*, the most powerful battleship on the face of the Earth. Unlike the dams, however, they needed four attacks to sink her. No. 617 Squadron's first crack at the *Tirpitz* was on 15 September 1944, and required them to operate from a Russian airfield in order to reach the battleship's anchorage at Kaa Fjord near the North Cape. The weapon used in the attack was the 12,000 lb Tallboy bomb, the largest bomb dropped from an aircraft up to that time. The attack was a failure because the Germans laid on a smokescreen in time to obscure the ship from all but the first Lancaster. One Lancaster was lost during the operation, and the Squadron returned to their base at Woodhall Spa in Lincolnshire.

The Germans subsequently moved the *Tirpitz* round the North Cape to a new anchorage at Tromsø Fjord on the west coast of Norway, which placed it just within reach of Lancasters operating from the very north of Scotland. The Lancasters still needed to be heavily modified for the operation. They had been re-equipped with more powerful Merlin 24 engines, replacing the Merlin 22s, and were greatly lightened by the removal of the pilot's armour plating, and the entire mid-upper gun turret. Large overload fuel tanks were then installed in the rear fuselage to give a total tankage of 2406 gallons for the 2250-mile round trip.

On 28 October 1944 the second Tallboy attack against *Tirpitz* got underway as thirty-six Lancasters eighteen each from No. 617 and No. 9 Squadrons took off from their bases at Woodhall Spa and Bardney. They flew north to RAF Lossiemouth and its satellite RAF Milltown, 4.5 miles north-east of Elgin, from where the attack would begin. The bombers brought their Tallboy bombs with them, and were ready to go as soon as they were refuelled, and provided weather conditions were suitable. A single aircraft from No. 463 Squadron was also to fly on the operation, carrying a film crew.

A Mosquito reconnaissance aircraft flew over the Fjord at around midnight and reported that the wind had changed round to the east and had blown away the low clouds over the target. By 01.00 hrs of the 29 October the Lancasters were taxiing out for take-off. Flying Officer Daniel William Carey DFC, an Australian, piloting Lancaster NF920, coded KC-E, took off at 01.14 hrs. E for Easy had been given the name *Easy Elsie* by the crew, with a suitably unclothed figure painted on the nose.

Carey was usually known as Bill, and was quite short for a bomber pilot. He had enlisted in the RAAF when he was 23 and done his elementary flying training in Australia. Arriving in Great Britain in August 1942, he had been through No. 15 Advanced Flying Unit and then No. 29 OTU. After crewing up and being converted to Lancasters, he had joined No. 106 Squadron at Metheringham in February 1944. After eleven operations with No. 106 Squadron his application to join No. 617 squadron was approved and he flew his first operation with them on the night of 18 – 19 April. The attack on the *Tirpitz* was his thirty-seventh operation.

There was also a Canadian in the crew, Pilot Officer Doug McLennan, the bomb-aimer. He had joined the RCAF in September 1941 and had trained initially as a pilot, but was eventually transferred to training as a bomb-aimer. After arriving in Great Britain in January 1943, he went to No. 5 Air Observers School, and then to No. 29 OTU, where he crewed up with Bill Carey. As part of Carey's crew he went with him to No. 617 Squadron. On the first attack on the *Tirpitz*, though positioned with the rest of the Squadron in Russia, *Easy Elsie* had been unable to take part in the attack, but Carey, McLennan and the rest of the crew flew the raid as passengers with other crews.

The rest of *Easy Elsie*'s crew was British. There were two other officers, Pilot Officer Alex McKie, the navigator, and Flying Officer GA Witherick DFM, the rear gunner. McKie had joined the RAF just before the War as an engineering apprentice at Halton, but in 1942 he had been accepted for pilot training. He did his elementary training at Syerston and then went to the United States for his advanced training. Unfortunately, he was thrown out of pilot training after an episode of unauthorised low flying, and was remustered for navigator training. Arriving back in his homeland, he went to No. 16 OTU and was crewed with an Australian pilot before going to No. 106 Squadron, where they completed a tour of thirty operations. The crew transferred to No. 617 Squadron in May 1944. When his pilot left, having completed a second tour, McKie flew with a number of other pilots, including Carey aboard *Easy Elsie*.

Gerry Witherick was a veteran of ninety-five operations. He had joined the RAF in 1936 and when War broke out was an LAC driver with No. 47 Squadron in the Sudan. A shortage of air gunners for their Wellesleys caused him to be given brief training, and then he began to fly on operations against the Italians in Eritrea. After two years in the Sudan he was posted to No. 70 Squadron flying Wellingtons in Egypt, and had to learn the intricacies of their Frazer-Nash 4-gun tail turrets.

After a total of thirty-seven operations in Africa, behind the hand-held Vickers guns of the Wellesleys or the power-operated Brownings of the

Wellingtons, he was transferred back to Great Britain, where he eventually found himself operating the Boulton Paul 4-gun turret in the tail of a No. 405 Squadron Halifax from RAF Pocklington. He flew twenty more operations, plus eleven patrols when attached to Coastal Command for a while, and was then assigned to a training establishment, which did not entirely suit him. He sent off his application to be posted to No. 617 Squadron, and was very pleased when it was accepted.

The other two crew members of *Easy Elsie* were Flight Sergeants, Les Franks, the flight engineer, and AE, 'Curly' Young, the wireless operator.

As the heavily laden bombers lumbered one by one into the air, the visibility over the Moray Firth was very poor. The plan was to cross Norway and then fly on into Swedish airspace. They intended to attack from the east, using the Swedish mountains as a radar shield, in an attempt to surprise the battleship's defences, though it was believed this did not this time include a smokescreen. Once Scotland and the Orkneys had been cleared they were to fly at 600 feet to stay below the German radar, and as they approached the centre of the Norwegian coast were to climb to a safety height of over 6000 feet to clear the mountains as they crossed into Swedish airspace.

Carey's crew followed this plan exactly, and as they swung north they flew over the Swedish villages of Suorva and Abisko, ready to rendezvous after dawn with the rest of the force over Lake Stora Lulevatten. The two squadrons would then turn north-west to attack in a loose formation and prepare to attack the battleship at the required height of 16,000 feet behind Wing Commander Tait's lead aircraft.

Easy Elsie arrived at the rendezvous on time, and the crew found themselves amongst a gaggle of circling Lancasters. Only Wing Commander Tait's aircraft did not appear, so when the time to turn for the target approached, the Number Two, Squadron Leader Gerry Fawke, fired a series of green Very cartridges and led the formation to the north-west. As the formation was sorting itself out on track, Tait's Lancaster came soaring over them to take up its allotted position at the head of the formation.

As Tromsø Fjord came into sight they could see *Tirpitz* quite clearly in the crystal clear air, but the wind must have changed because the clouds were swinging back over the target area.

As Carey approached the battleship, its huge battery of anti-aircraft guns, including its 15-inch main armament, as well as the shore batteries, opened fire. All was going well but then Doug McLennan announced that *Tirpitz* was obscured by cloud, and Carey took the Lancaster round again for a second bomb-run. As he did so there was a huge shell burst only just below them, but no damage seemed to result. On the second run, they had no better luck than the first, as cloud still obscured the target and so Carey took the aircraft round on a third bombing run. All the time the anti-aircraft fire was bursting in the sky around them, and suddenly a shell exploded to the right, shaking the whole aircraft. Les Franks, looking out, could see they had been hit in the starboard wing, puncturing a fuel tank, and a stream of fuel was flowing from the wing.

As Carey manoeuvred the aircraft for a third run, he was aware that there were several other Lancasters milling around in the sky as well, all trying to find the moment when the battleship below was clear of cloud as they made their bombing run. Their Stabilized Automatic Bomb-Sight (SABS) required a precise speed and altitude, as well as inputs for the wind and the outside air temperature, all of which needed a long run up to the target. However, if SABS was set up right, and the flying was precise enough, the Tallboy could be placed within 20 yards of the aiming point; not quite a pickle barrel, but good enough for the earthquake effect of the 12,000 lb bomb to have its effect.

For a third time Carey was forced to turn away, and then for a fourth and fifth time he took *Easy Elsie* round and brought her back in on a bombing run. Each time, the target was obscured by cloud. On the sixth run their luck changed, as *Tirpitz* was visible for the whole of the run. A wave of relief filled the aircraft as Doug McLennan called 'Bomb gone!' However, their joy did not last for long.

As Bill Carey turned the aircraft to the west, *Easy Elsie* shuddered as she was hit again, and then shuddered once more as another shell struck. Les Franks immediately reported that the port inner engine had stopped, and that there was heavy fuel loss from the port wing, as Bill Carey feathered the propeller. From the rear turret Gerry Witherick reported that their Tallboy had scored a hit or a near miss on the battleship. Carey found he could not shut the bomb doors, the loss of the port inner had caused loss of hydraulic power to them, and that would also mean the undercarriage could not be hydraulically extended, though the mainwheels could still be blown down with the emergency pneumatic system.

Their briefing had called for an immediate dive to 1000 feet after bombing, to clear the area quickly, and Carey had the nose of the aircraft down flying to the west. He saw a small town on an island and decided to fly across it to give them a good navigational fix for the return across the North Sea. As they overflew it the island exploded with anti-aircraft fire. The aircraft was hit again, and a large hole was blasted in the fuselage next to the wireless operator's position, putting the radio out of action. Luckily for Curly Young he had just left his position to use the Elsan.

As they took stock of their situation, the starboard outer engine began to run rough. Les Franks worked out that they had lost about 800 gallons of fuel and there was no longer enough left for them to make the long return flight across the North Sea. They had two choices, to turn back and make for Sweden, or to try and ditch near one of the Royal Navy destroyers that had been positioned on track for just such an emergency. Carey tried to contact the destroyers on the VHF set, but there was no response. He was concerned that with their fuel loss they would not have a great margin for finding one of the destroyers, and he was uncertain of the ditching characteristics of a Lancaster with the bomb doors down. He did not want to have to spend much time in the waters of the North Sea in late October, even if they could survive the ditching, and get in the dinghy. He informed the crew that he had decided to try and make a forced landing in Sweden. The crew were all in agreement and the only problem seemed to be that they would need to climb to 6000 feet to cross the mountain range again.

They tried and failed to contact other aircraft on the VHF set and then Alex McKie began firing red Very cartridges to try and attract the attention of any other Lancasters that were still around. This brought an immediate agitated response from Witherick in the rear turret, who could see the flares exploding very near to the trail of fuel still coming from the wing. Mckie immediately desisted and began planning their route to Sweden. However, the flares had been seen by Flight Lieutenant Hamilton who was just leaving Tromsø and he called on his VHF to find out what the problem was. Carey was able to brief Hamilton on their situation and that they were resigned to internment in Sweden.

Les Franks was busy transferring all the fuel he could to undamaged tanks, and Carey ordered Witherick to stay in the rear turret to look out for fighters. Everyone else was ordered to chuck out everything they did not need. They did all they could to lighten the aircraft. The guns and ammunition from the front turret were unceremoniously thrown overboard, together with the useless wireless set, their parachutes, the F9 camera, after the film had been exposed, and even the Gee set after a few taps with an axe.

Carey put the aircraft into a climb and headed up the Malangay Inlet. They were very grateful when the altimeter needle slid slowly past 6000 feet. Soon afterwards, they were flying over Lake Kilpisjarvi where the borders of Norway, Sweden and Finland meet. They then turned south-west in the direction of Porjus, one of the scarce towns in Lapland, where they hoped to make their forced landing. Les Franks worked out that it would take about 36 minutes to get there, and that they had 50 minutes' of fuel, if the gauges were reading correctly. They would not have much of a margin for error, or hesitation.

Once McKie was certain they were well inside Swedish airspace they began shredding their maps and code books. McKie kept the maps of the local area, and was checking their route against the ground below. Once they were over Lake Stora Lulevatten once more they decided to ditch the guns and ammunition from the rear turret. As they flew down the long thin lake the guns, gun-sight and ammo splashed into its placid waters.

The area was heavily forested and Carey commenced a wide sweep to look for a possible landing place, while beginning to lose height. They spotted a long grassy area running down to the lake, and decided it would be foolish to ignore what looked like a reasonable bet, and go searching for something better. They made a low pass over the area, and Carey decided that it looked so good he would try a wheels-down landing. He asked Les Franks to stay beside him to put the wheels down with the emergency pneumatic bottles, while the others took up their crash positions facing aft behind the main spar.

Carey made a wide flat circuit of the clearing and brought the crippled Lancaster in towards it. When they were nicely lined up he called Franks to lower the undercarriage and they were both relieved to see the green lights showing the wheels were down and locked. The flight engineer did not have the time to make his crash position behind the main spar so he quickly strapped himself into the second pilot's seat. As Carey levelled off and cut the throttles, Franks pushed the buttons to set off the fire extinguishers in all the engines.

The aircraft touched down, and then almost seemed to stop dead. The mainwheels dug into the marshy ground and stood the aircraft on its nose turret. With mud swamping in through the broken nose Les Franks shot out of his seat and through the windscreen and made a soft landing outside in the marsh. Bill Carey was thrust forward against his straps, and despite having pulled them as tight as he could, his knee hit the compass, which dislocated the knee cap. Luckily, the aircraft did not somersault and crashed back onto its tail.

The five crew members who were still in the aircraft sat immobile for a moment shocked by the sudden deceleration and the silence. Bill Carey was surprised to see Les Franks outside the aircraft waving to him, and wondered how he had got there so quickly. The four in the back were just disentangling themselves from their harnesses ready to exit the aircraft when Bill Carey informed them over the intercom that he had injured his knee and could not get out. They clambered forward to the cockpit to help him out, and as they were helping him over the spar, became concerned that Les Franks was not there. They called his name, and he yelled that he was outside in the marsh.

Between them they carried Carey out of the aircraft and then splashed away from the aircraft as quickly as they could. They were fairly certain that the aircraft would not catch fire, because of the low fuel state, but were anxious not to take chances. Their feet sank completely into the bog as they walked for the first thirty yards and they carried on for a further fifty until they could put their pilot down on a wooded slope. Gerry had carried a parachute pack from the aircraft, which had somehow not been jettisoned, and now wrapped Carey in the silk.

McKie and McLennan now tried to destroy the aircraft as per standing instructions, using the four incendiary charges provided, which they inserted two in each wing. They noticed that the wheel-tracks of the aircraft only ran for about twenty yards, as the mainwheels completely buried themselves. They retreated from the aircraft to wait for the charges to go off, but nothing happened. They returned to the aircraft and punctured the intact petrol tanks. Before setting fire to it, they pulled the dinghy release handle, but nothing happened. It had been a good decision not to attempt ditching in the sea.

McKie made a torch from one of his last surviving maps and tossed it into the petrol, and as they ran away as fast as they could in the sticky swamp the aircraft went up in flames. Soon Very cartridges and odd rounds of ammunition were going off, and then suddenly the dinghy shot from the wing, and began inflating. They sat together by the trees and watched *Easy Elsie* being consumed by the flames, though only the centre fuselage was actually burning.

Once the fire began to die down they had to decide what to do next. The weather was sunny and fairly warm for the time of the year, but they did not think they could remain where they were and hope the locals would have noticed the fire and come and looking for them. Besides, Bill Carey needed to be taken to hospital to have his knee fixed. It was decided that McKie and Young would go for help, but before they went the survival rations were fetched from the dinghy. They were shocked to discover that they only consisted of a few tins of water, as had Petrie-Andrews' Halifax crew floating in the Mediterranean the year before. Speculating about what had happened to the rations that should have been there was not helpful, but going for help was now even more imperative.

McKie and Young walked the short distance to the lake and then began moving south along its edge. Before long they came to a boat-house, and inside were a number of boats. They chose a small one and rowed to the other side of the lake, where they beached the boat safely, and headed for a railway line McKie had seen from the air. When they found it they walked along the tracks southwards towards the town of Porjus.

On the outskirts of the town they knocked on the door of the first house they came to. McKie started to speak when an old lady opened the door, but then she slammed it in their faces. At the next house they received a warmer welcome from a younger lady who invited them inside, speaking good English. She gave them something to eat and drink while she went to contact the authorities.

Not long afterwards a Swedish Army lorry drew up and took them into the town, and put them in the local prison. They told the officer in charge about their colleagues and pointed out where they thought they had landed on a map. A party with a stretcher was sent to find them.

The others were a little wary when they heard approaching voices, not entirely sure what sort of reception they would receive, and even a little unsure if the Germans ever penetrated this far across the border. After all, they themselves had violated Swedish airspace only a few hours before on an operational mission.

They need not have worried of course, they were treated with great kindness and even enthusiasm. The Royal Air Force was definitely popular in Sweden at the time, and though they did not reveal any details of their mission, everyone knew what they were doing there. There were not all that many targets in northern Norway worthy of a major effort. *Tirpitz* had survived the attack, though there had been a number of near misses. No. 617 Squadron staged a repeat of the attack on 13 November, once more staging through Scotland and heading for Norway. This time several of the Tallboys struck home, and the great battleship turned over and sank.

Though the Swedes knew the Lancasters were probably trying to attack *Tirpitz*, they were a little concerned that they might have also been trying to bomb the dam on Stora Lulevatten. However, the crew reassured them that the splashes that had been witnessed were only equipment being jettisoned to lighten the aircraft for the final landing.

The formation had been seen gathering over the lake earlier in the morning, but Carey's crew were able to explain it as a navigational error by the leader, which he had rectified as soon as he realised by firing a number of flares, and leading them out of Swedish airspace as soon as possible. Whether the Swedes believed this or not, is unrecorded.

Bill Carey had been taken to the small hospital that served Porjus, but after initial treatment he was taken to the much larger hospital at Yokkmukk. He and his crew were not to meet up again until they got back to Britain, where they could swap notes and memories about their short, and not entirely unagreeable, Swedish holiday.

Unlike aircrew who had been shot down over occupied Europe, and had evaded capture or had escaped, Carey's crew were able to go back onto operations. By the end of the War Carey himself had flown another eleven operations, including one dropping of the 22,000 lb Grand Slam bomb, aimed by Doug McLennan on the U-Boat pens at Farge, part of the Hamburg port complex. Gerry Witherick achieved his 'century', a total of 104 bombing operations, not including five early returns and the eleven patrols with Coastal Command. All of them became keen post-War members of the 617 Squadron Association.

Easy Elsie lay where she was. Only the central section of the fuselage was burnt out, the outer wings, tail, and the rest of the fuselage lay where they had fallen. The Swedes took away the engines, and any other useful equipment, but the rest of *Easy Elsie* remained as a long-term reminder of Porjus's unexpected visitors.

59. Carey's Lancaster *Easy Elsie*, still lying on the tundra in northern Sweden in 1958.

CHAPTER 19

Down in the Peak District

Sometimes, the difference between a crash-landing and a crash is only in the intent of the pilot, the result turns out just the same. If the crew do not survive, as with James Craig's Defiant crash in 1941 (see Chapter 12), there is no way of knowing if a forced landing was intended or not. In 1945 Ted Croker, later to become famous as the Secretary of the Football Association, was a pilot learning to fly Airspeed Oxfords at RAF Seighford near Stafford. On 28 December he was involved in a crash, rather than a crash-landing, on Brown Knoll in the Peak District, high above Edale, but survived to explain what had happened, and was later able to play football again.

Edgar Alfred Croker, known as Ted, was born in Kingston upon Thames. At the beginning of the War he was 15 years old and at Kingston Technical College. When he left he got a job as a draughtsman at the Andre Rubber Company at Tolworth. He moved to Hawker Aircraft at Kingston upon Thames, helping to design tools for the production of the Typhoon. Despite being in a reserved occupation he volunteered for the Royal Air Force, becoming part of Intake No. 52 at Lord's Cricket Ground, of all places.

After a disillusioning period billeted in St. John's Wood, he went for his initial training to Newquay, Cornwall. When this was completed he was shunted around the country to different establishments at Heaton Park and Brighton, before boarding a troopship on the Clyde. His destination was Durban, South Africa.

He was to spend two and a half years in South Africa, firstly as a pupil pilot then as an instructor. His elementary flying training was on Tiger Moths at Randfontein near Johannesburg. His advanced training was on Harvards at Vereeniging, south of Johannesburg. He was presented with his wings, and promoted to pilot officer, in November 1943.

Like many newly qualified pupil pilots he then served as a flying instructor in South Africa, teaching new intakes the rudiments of their new profession. It was not until late in 1945 that he finally returned to England, and a posting to No. 21 (Pilots) Advanced Flying Unit at RAF Wheaton Aston, near Stafford.

60. Ted Croker just before the crash.

This unit specialised in acclimatising pilots trained in the sunny climes of Southern Africa and North America to European weather and flying conditions, and in many cases their conversion to twin-engined aircraft. By 1945 it was a huge operation, and Wheaton Aston was said to be, for a while, the busiest airfield in Britain. It was necessary for the unit to be assigned satellite airfields at Tatenhill, Perton and Seighford, and there were over 120 Airspeed Oxfords on strength. Ted Croker was one of the thousands of pilots who passed through its hands, having returned from South Africa, though the War had by now finished, and there were the first signs that its operations were being run down.

Ted Croker had been promoted again to flying officer, and was flying from Wheaton Aston's satellite at RAF Seighford, an airfield 5 miles west of Stafford. It was originally built as a satellite to the Wellington bomber OTU at Hixon. Despite his posting in the Midlands he had been taken on the books of Charlton Athletic Football Club and when weekend passes permitted, he played a couple of reserve games for them. However, his flying career was shortly to put an end to his playing career for quite some time.

On the afternoon of Friday, 29 December 1945, Croker, strolled out to Airspeed Oxford HN594, along with Flying Officer John Dowthwaite, who had also been trained in South Africa. With them was Warrant Officer George 'Robbie' Robinson, pilot and navigator instructor, who was going to lead them on a low-level map-reading test, intending to fly over the area of Robinson's home-town, Sheffield.

Even though it was very cold, they only wore their normal battledress clothing, for they would not be flying at any great altitude, and the Oxford cabin was heated. It was a dismal day, with total cloud cover and showers in the air as they walked along the perimeter track to the parked aircraft, carrying their parachutes.

The camouflaged Oxford was a war-weary aircraft, built by the parent company at Portsmouth, but should have been well able to complete the task they had planned. John Dowthwaite took the left hand, first pilot's, seat, and Robinson sat alongside him. The right hand seat could be slid back to allow room to unfold a small map table, which he duly did, and laid out a map of the Pennine district. He marked on it a triangular course that he was going to ask them to follow. They had not filed a flight plan before climbing aboard the aircraft, so the Station did not know the route they would be taking.

Ted Croker sat behind the other two, on a seat that straddled the main spar. He would only be observing for the first part of the flight. Robinson flew the plane and for the first leg to the north-east Dowthwaite map-read his way across Staffordshire and Derbyshire, and into Yorkshire. Then he and Croker changed places for a short 15–20 mile leg going almost due west. Ted Croker did not bother to strap himself in once more when he changed places, which was to have significant consequences shortly afterwards.

The weather was much worse with the cloud base reaching down to the ground, forcing Robinson to climb. The climbing rate of the old Oxford was not good, it was beginning to show how war-weary it was. Then Croker noticed that ice was beginning to form on the wing, which only made matters worse. Looking at his map he noticed that Kinder Scout, which was in the immediate area, was 2088 ft and they were now flying level at only 2000 feet. He expressed his concern to Robinson, who told him not to worry because he knew the area like the back of his hand.

At that moment the cloud became distinctly solid, and at 120 mph the Oxford was crashing across the rough moorland of Brown Knoll, disintegrating around them in a crashing, splintering wreck of wood, metal and peat.

All three men were knocked unconscious immediately as the aircraft crashed and slid to a halt in about 50 yards, disintegrating completely. This was not a crash-landing of course. It was not a landing of any kind, it was a crash pure and simple; but they had struck the hillside very near the summit at a very low angle, and the effect was much as if they had intended a wheels-up crash landing.

61. The port wing of the Oxford lying on the moor.

Croker regained consciousness sometime later. He was lying on the ground about 50 feet from the wreck, where he had been flung because he had not been strapped in. He was freezing cold, and there was severe pain in his two ankles. He thought at first that he was dreaming and shut his eyes to return to sleep, but the pain and cold did not go away. Then he became aware of voices coming from the shattered wreckage.

He recovered his senses and crawled on his hands and knees to where the other two lay. It was clear that they were both in a far worse condition. Robinson had both legs broken and a splintered jaw, and Dowthwaite also had broken legs. Looking around the desolate, mist-shrouded, moorland, with patches of snow lying in all the hollows, it was clear that rescue would not be swift. No one knew the route they were taking and it would be sometime before they were reported overdue. Though it was only 2.30 pm, mid-winter darkness would be falling soon, precluding an air-search until the following day. Dressed as they were in their ordinary battledress, it was doubtful if they would survive the night. As the least severely injured, having luckily been thrown well clear of the wreck, because he was not strapped in, Ted Croker soon realised that it was he who would have to go for help.

The parachutes had opened on impact and he wrapped these round his two companions. He had lost his shoes in the crash, and the seat of his trousers had also been ripped off.

He asked Robinson which direction he should take, as he had claimed to know the area well. He set off on the way Robbie had vaguely pointed, attempting to walk at first, but the pain in his badly sprained ankles was too much, and he resorted to crawling on all fours. For no real reason, after a short way he changed direction by ninety degrees, and made slow progress on his hands and knees, or by sliding downhill on his bottom.

The shock of the crash and the bitterly cold weather took their toll and the dank mist soaked him through, the moisture beginning to freeze. He was desperately anxious to lie down and go to sleep. However, he knew that if he did, he might well die of exposure on the moor, and then so would his two companions. He saw some sheep and even began crawling towards them, hoping to grab one to share its woolly warmth, but this absurd idea soon withered as the sheep took fright, and ran away.

The ground began falling away steeply, which was a good sign, as long as he was not crawling into a valley from which he would later have to climb out. As he crawled and slid down below the cloud cover he found himself in a valley with a stream flowing through it, flooded by the winter rains. Beyond the stream were two cottages, one of which had the Youth Hostels Association symbol on the wall. As he watched, a man left this building and walked away. Croker yelled repeatedly but his voice was weak and the man did not hear. Desperately hoping that the man was not the only occupant of the cottages, Croker struggled across the stream, which was brown from the peat. He made his way to the first cottage. which was the Youth Hostel. He knocked as loudly as he could on the door. There was no answer, and he guessed that it was closed for the Winter.

He struggled to the other small cottage and knocked on that door. It was opened by an old lady, who he later discovered was named Mrs Shirt. He must have looked a shocking sight, a tattered figure on his knees in her doorway, in the remains of his RAF battledress, covered from bare head to bare feet in blood and mud. 'Look, I am sorry to trouble you, but I need some help,' he said with astonishing understatement, 'There are two of my colleagues up on the hill.'

The RAF wings on the remains of his battledress were all the explanation that was needed by Mrs Shirt. The Dark Peak had claimed another aircraft, one of well over fifty which came down there. She invited him in and explained that she would have to go for the police as now that her son had left she was the only one left up there. At his request she fetched a bowl of hot water in which he could soak his feet. As he sank into a chair and placed them gratefully in it the blood swirled around in the water. After she had gone, walking the mile to the village of Edale, Croker's tiredness and shock finally overcame him and he fell asleep.

He had somehow descended a mile and a half from near the summit of Brown Knoll. He had clambered across the snow-spotted moorland on all fours and sliding down a very steep hillside, descending almost 1000 feet, and across the stream known as Grain Clough, to Lee Farm.

Mrs Shirt telephoned the police at Chapel Milton, who in turn telephoned RAF Harpur Hill where the call was taken at 5.20 pm. Within twenty minutes their mountain rescue team was on its way.

When Croker awoke he was lying in an ambulance outside the cottage. A doctor and some volunteers had been up the hillside but had no success at finding the wreck, though it later transpired that they had been within 50 yards of it in the darkness. They decided that they had to wake him up so he could tell them where it was. He gave them what directions he could and when the mountain rescue team arrived they continued the search until 3 am. The team was led by Flight Lieutenant David 'Doc' Crichton, who as medical officer at 28 MU at Harpur Hill had been responsible, in 1942, for organising the RAF Mountain Rescue team there, which covered the area of the Peak District. His team attended over forty crashes during the remaining three years of the War, though it had never been recognised in Air Ministry Orders as a Mountain Rescue Unit; as had teams in other parts of the country, something for which Crichton was most bitter. Nevertheless, in January 1946 he was to be awarded the MBE in recognition of his efforts, and he later reached the rank of Air Commodore.

His team split up and spread out across the hillside, towing sledge stretchers on which they could bring down the two injured men. They fired flares at regular intervals, and it turned out later that they passed within 400 yards of the wreck without seeing it in the darkness and mist. They covered about 20 square miles of moorland searching Edale Head, Jacob's Ladder and Green Clough. When a sledge fell over a ravine, they were forced to call off the search until the morning.

Ted Croker was taken down the hill to hospital and then moved to the RAF hospital at Wombwell. His head wound, caused when he was thrown through the windscreen of the Oxford, required eighty-eight stitches. However, there was one small positive outcome to the episode. While in South Africa he had lost a tooth playing football and had had a replacement installed held by gold caps on each side. He hated the appearance of the gold caps and was glad to see they had been knocked out in the crash. He took the opportunity to have them crowned again without the gold.

The search for the wreck resumed again at first light, rockets being fired to let the poor men on the moor know that help was on the way. The searchers eventually found the wreck at 10 am. Both men were still alive, though frostbitten, and very relieved to see that Ted Croker had brought them help. After twenty hours of lying on the freezing moorland, the two men were carried down by stretcher for about a mile to a point where Crichton had managed to get his jeeps. The jeeps relayed them down the moor and they were taken by ambulance to the RAF hospital at Wilmslow,

62. The tangled wreckage of the Oxford as it was when the rescue team found the crash site. It's hard to believe anyone survived.

Cheshire. Because of the frostbite it was deemed necessary to amputate Robinson's broken leg.

Because Ted Croker had been able to go for help they had survived their ordeal. In contrast, Flying Officer Craig, and LAC Hempstead, the two men in the Defiant crash four years earlier, and fewer than 8 miles away to the north, had had to wait for rescue. They had not survived, even though their ordeal had been in the middle of summer. The Dark Peak can be a forbidding and dangerous place at any time of year.

After Ted Croker recovered from his injuries, spending some time at the aircrew rehabilitation centre at Loughborough College, he signed professional forms for Charlton Athletic in 1948. However, he was only to play eight first-team games for them in the season 1950–51. Shortly afterwards, he was called back to the RAF because of the Korean War, and did not play for Charlton again. After his return to civvie street he played in the Southern League for three seasons, but a severely fractured leg put an end to his football career in 1956.

Before becoming Secretary of the Football Association he developed a

63. The rescue team bringing down one of the three survivors.

successful business career, and during this period he had a frightening echo of his crash in the Peak District. He had sold his Company to Liner Concrete, whose head office was in Gateshead. He became a director of the parent company and needed to make frequent trips to the north east. Occasionally, he hired a light aircraft, if there was any need for haste. His Private Pilot's Licence had lapsed so he had to hire the owner-pilot as well as his aircraft.

On about the third occasion he hired the aircraft to take him from Staverton Airport in Gloucestershire to Newcastle Airport they were flying over the Pennines in cloud that reached down to the hill-tops. Suddenly, the engine gave a frightening cough. Memories of his previous experience flashed before him, and the adrenalin pumped into his veins. The pilot switched fuel tanks, but the engine continued to splutter. Then Croker's wartime training came into use, as he looked round for the trouble. He noticed that the outside air temperature thermometer was reading zero and they were flying in cloud, the perfect conditions for carburettor icing. He suggested to the pilot that it might be a good idea to switch on his carburettor heat, and when he did so the engine soon smoothed out.

He then demanded that the pilot fly due East until radio beacons told them they were over low ground, and then descend below cloud cover. After a while they spotted a hole in the clouds and dived down, finding themselves in one of the Pennine valleys that run eastwards. They flew east until they could turn north once more, keeping below clouds all the way to Newcastle.

Some years later, the three men who had survived that winter night on Brown Knoll, Ted Croker, George Robinson, and John Dowthwaite, climbed back up together to the site of their crash. They reflected on how lucky they had been, when so many others had perished on those desolate moors. They drank a toast to their own survival.

4. Ted Croker returning to the air in the 1950s, in a de Havilland Chipmunk.

CHAPTER 20

What You Do When the Engine Falls Off

There have been a number of recorded occasions when engines have fallen off aircraft in flight, only for the pilot to make a successful forced landing, but almost all were multi-engined aircraft. For this to happen to a single-engined aircraft, and for all aboard to survive unscathed, would require a remarkable conjunction of favourable conditions. An aircraft with excellent low-speed handling, with a highly experienced test pilot at the controls, would help enormously.

Robin Lindsay Neale was born on 24 January 1912, and was educated at Caterham. He first became connected with aviation when he worked for Selfridge's Aviation Department. He later worked for Brian Lewis & Co. at Heston. In 1931 he learned to fly at Croydon, getting his 'A' Licence. After a short period of working with Chamier, Gilbert Lodge & Co., in 1935 he set up his own aviation consultancy business, under the name Lindsay Neale Aviation Ltd. He was Managing Director, and he owned his own Puss Moth.

He also became a director of Dart Aircraft Ltd, test-flying their single-seat light aircraft, and undertaking other freelance testing. Among the aircraft he flew during the 1930s was one of the de Havilland Comets. During this time, when he was only 19, he broke his pelvis in a motorbike accident, which left him with a permanent limp, as his right leg was slightly twisted and shortened. At the outbreak of the War he closed his business and joined the RAF, but was released to work as a test pilot for Boulton

65. Robin Lindsay Neale about to test-fly a Blackburn Roc in 1940.

Paul Aircraft Ltd, arriving on 1 January 1940. At the time Boulton Paul was building both Blackburn Rocs and its own Defiant, and later built Fairey Barracudas.

He was a well-liked character in the factory, and was fond of a practical joke. Rather than fly a Defiant or Barracuda solo, he would often offer people in the flight shed area a 'quick flight' in lieu of ballast. His 'quick flight' would then involve him wringing every aerobatic manoeuvre from the airframe that it would manage. The volunteer 'rear gunner', would emerge looking very green indeed, and sometimes worse than that.

His regular daily task was the flight-testing of new Defiants and Rocs, and later on Barracudas as they rolled off the production line. The more advanced testing of new developments was usually done by the chief test pilot, Cecil Feather. The taxiway, which ran from the flights sheds at the rear of the factory round the corner of Pendeford Hill to the airfield, Wolverhampton Airport, was well used in both directions and this had unfortunate consequences in July 1940.

On the 27th at about 11.05 am, Cecil Feather was taxiing out in the prototype of the Mark II Defiant, N1550. The aircraft had had its first flight only seven days before, and was the first stage in a programme to give the Defiant a much-needed power increase. At exactly the same time, Lindsay Neale was taxiing a production Defiant Mark I, N1639, from the airfield,

66. Robin Lindsay Neale about to test-fly a Defiant, with some of the Boulton Paul flight shed crew.

where he had just landed after a test flight, down the taxiway back to the flight sheds. The two collided head on, severely damaging both aircraft. Neither pilot was hurt, but the two 'gunners', providing ballast in the turrets, both received minor injuries, and had to be taken to the Royal Hospital.

The incident would have been amusing except for these injuries, and the fact that the accident delayed the Defiant Mark II development programme by several weeks. The second prototype Mark II, N1551, was not ready until later in the summer. Very sharp letters were received from the Air Ministry.

Lindsay Neale's first experience of a crash-landing came in 1941 when he was flying an old Boulton Paul Overstrand. The Overstrand, K8176, had been retained by the company for turret development work, having the prototype Defiant turret and then a SAMM 20 mm cannon mounting in the nose, replacing its own pneumatic turret. On 30 May 1941 the aircraft, newly camouflaged with the paint still wet, took off from Wolverhampton on a flight to Edinburgh, with Lindsay Neale at the controls, and Slim Bunkell, Boulton Paul's flight shed foreman, as the only passenger. As they neared Blackpool they found themselves in a thunderstorm, and so Lindsay Neale decided it was prudent to land at Squires Gate.

As they were coming in to land the aircraft was struck by lightning, and Lindsay Neale, blinded by the flash, landed offset and not on the runway. The aircraft toppled into a ditch and crumpled into a heap. The sudden shock of the thunder, the flash and the crash scared the living daylights out of Slim, and Lindsay Neale found him in the wreckage with his hands over his eyes saying 'Old Nick's got me at last'. As a postscript to the crash, a more accurate description than a crash-landing, someone sent Lindsay Neale's wife, Rosemary, the 'remains' of the aircraft in a matchbox – just a piece of the fabric.

With the retirement of the chief test pilot, Cecil Feather in 1945, possibly through illness brought on by stress, Lindsay Neale was promoted to his position. The company was then in the process of overhauling 270 Wellington bombers and converting them to T10 navigation trainers. Having to fly Wellingtons, rather than the slightly more agile Barracudas or Defiants, only partially curtailed Lindsay Neale's penchant for aerobatics. While demonstrating one at an air show at Wolverhampton Airport in 1948, he did a low and very fast pass at about 20 feet across the airfield and then pulled it up into a loop! When he landed, everything loose inside the aircraft, was rattling around. Everything that should have been hung up was dangling down and all the acid had run from the batteries!

While the Boulton Paul factory was full of Wellingtons the company was developing its Balliol advanced trainer. The Balliol was designed to Spec. T.7/45, which called for a turboprop three-seat advanced trainer, to replace the wartime Harvards and Masters. The Balliol was ordered in prototype form, with either the Rolls-Royce Dart or the Armstrong-Siddeley Mamba turboprop engine. However, slow progress with both engines led to the decision to fit a Bristol Mercury radial to the first Balliol prototype to undertake early flight testing.

On 30 May 1947 the Balliol prototype, VL892, took off on its first flight with Lindsay Neale at the controls. He flew from the grass runways of Wolverhampton Airport, alongside the Boulton Paul factory. The aircraft proved a lovely aircraft to fly, though rather underpowered with the Mercury.

A few weeks later, while the second prototype Balliol, VL917, was being fitted with a Mamba, which was more advanced in its development than the Dart, Lindsay Neale took his family off on a summer holiday to the south of France. He borrowed a Miles Messenger, G-AJEY, from Miles Aircraft, and with his wife, Rosemary, sister-in-law, Hazel, and children, Jenny and Jeff, took off for the flight across the Channel and south over France.

On 28 June they had reached south-eastern France, near the town of Bait, and were cruising along at 4000 feet. Lindsay Neale was dozing in the front passenger seat, with Hazel, then only 19, in the pilot's seat. Jenny, only 3, was on her lap. Suddenly, there was a huge bang. The aircraft reared up into an alarmingly steep angle and there was a total loss of power. Lindsay Neale woke up with a start, and automatically grabbed the stick and pushed it right forward before the aircraft stalled, still not entirely clear what had happened.

68. **Below Miles Messenger G-AJEY after Lindsay Neale's 'engine-off' landing.**

69. **Left Close-up of the Messenger's fireproof bulkhead, showing the broken engine mountin**

Hazel handed young Jenny back to her mother in the rear seat, who then hauled Hazel back with them. This was definitely not the thing to do as Lindsay Neale was fighting to hold the aircraft level, so he put on full flap, and ordered everyone to pile into the front seat, and to haul the baggage forward too. Luckily, his wife had packed everything into an old parachute bag, which was far handier to heave forward than a suitcase would have been.

The centre of gravity, though still further aft than it should have been on a Miles Messenger, was now in a more manageable position, and Lindsay Neale had enough control to glide down and begin to look for a field in which to make a forced landing. They were now aware that there did not seem to be much aircraft forward of the windscreen, which explained the sudden silence. They no longer seemed to have an engine. Lindsay Neale still had the control column right forward, but was able to affect a controlled landing in a field just large enough. They scrambled thankfully out, and examined the aircraft.

They discovered that the fixed pitch, one-piece, wooden propeller had cracked and one blade had broken off. The massive out-of-balance forces had torn the Gipsy Major engine from the airframe, complete with its mountings and cowlings. It was lucky that the aircraft was a Messenger, which had marvellous low-speed handling qualities, and that such an experienced test pilot was at the controls, who could react calmly and logically. It gave new meaning to the nautical expression 'Finished with engine'.

As a memento of this alarming experience the Miles Aircraft Company presented Lindsay Neale with a model of the Messenger – The Messenger involved, G-AJEY, was considered beyond repair.

I imagine test pilots take holidays to get away from such excitement, but

70. The model Messenger presented to Lindsay Neale by the Miles Aircraft, together with the propeller blade that broke off and the aircraft featuring on the cover of *Aeroplane Monthly*.

Lindsay Neale did not settle into a quiet life even on his return. The second prototype Balliol was nearing completion, with its Mamba engine, and Boulton Paul was in competition with Avro, and its Athena, to fly the world's first single-engined turboprop aircraft. On 24 May 1948 Balliol VL917, with Lindsay Neale at the controls, won the race, making its first flight, but it ended in a disastrous crash-landing.

Lindsay Neale was bringing VL917 in to land at Wolverhampton, and was letting down over the eastern end of the airfield when the propeller disced. With the blades acting as air brakes, the aircraft fell out of the sky. All would have been well if the undercarriage had not just clipped the iron railings along Marsh Lane, the boundary to the airfield, which caused the aircraft to crash and to break into several pieces. Lindsay Neale broke his leg in the crash in the same place it had been broken before the War. It was an ignominious end to a historic aircraft. By coincidence, a Boulton Paul photographer, Jack Endean, had filmed the aircraft on take-off, and began filming again a second before the crash, capturing a remarkable piece of film.

The crash did not affect the Balliol programme, as the decision had already been made to power production Balliols with war-surplus Merlin engines, which were far cheaper and more reliable than the early turboprops. With Lindsay Neale still recovering from his broken leg, the first flight of the first Merlin-powered prototype, VW897, was made by his assistant, Peter Tisshaw. Kingsley Peter Henry Tisshaw had been born in Putney on 25 September 1923, and was educated at St Paul's School and Aberdeen University. In 1941 he joined the RAF and received his flying

67. The Mamba-engined Boulton Paul Balliol T1 after its first flight crash, clipping the railings seen in the background on landing.

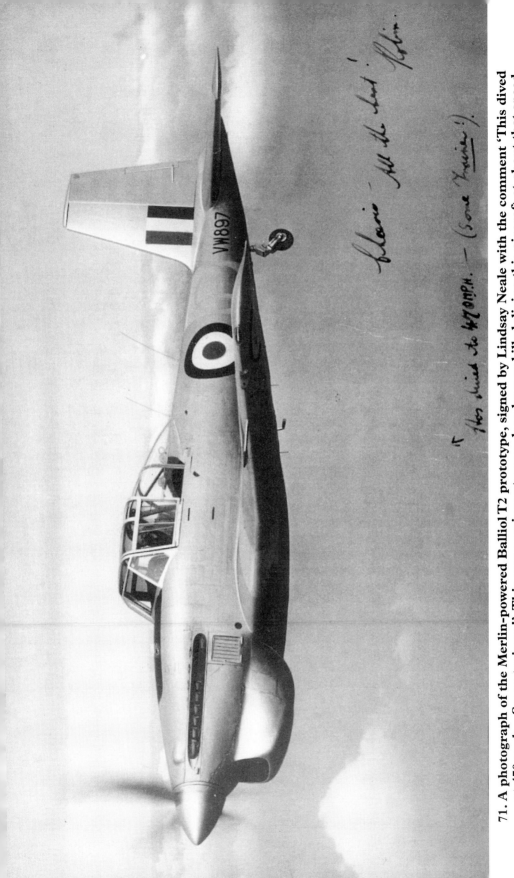

Please – all the best! Robin.

This dived to 470M.P.H. – (Some Trainer!).

71. A photograph of the Merlin-powered Balliol T2 prototype, signed by Lindsay Neale with the comment 'This dived at 470 mph – Some trainer !' This was a poignant remark as he was killed diving this aircraft at about that speed.

training in the United States. From 1942 he spent three years as a flying instructor at various stations in Great Britain, before being posted to Turkey in December 1947. He was demobilised in January 1947, and after taking his 'B' Licence he joined Boulton Paul as assistant to Lindsay Neale, as a replacement for Flight Lieutenant John O Lancaster, who had moved on to Saunders-Roe, and later Armstrong Whitworth. Tisshaw's main duties were flight-testing the Wellington T10s before delivery. He took over the Balliol testing while Lindsay Neale was recovering, and demonstrated the aircraft at Farnborough.

When Lindsay Neale had recovered, having had his leg set properly this time, he rejoined the testing programme. In particular, he tried to solve a control problem that had arisen. It was found that elevator reversal occurred when 320 mph was exceeded in an out-of-trim dive. On the afternoon of 3 February he took off with Peter Tisshaw to examine this problem and undertook a dive in the region of 400 mph from around 14,000 feet. The windscreen of VW897 disintegrated, possibly because of a bird strike, and the aircraft crashed at Coven not far from the airfield, killing both pilots.

Robin Lindsay Neale is remembered by all who knew him as a charming and friendly man, with a marvellous sense of humour. He was an accomplished test pilot, and a great loss to the company.

CHAPTER 21

To Bale Out or
Not to Bale Out

When something goes wrong in the air, pilots are often faced with making the decision of whether to try to land the aircraft, or to bale out. This is only usually an option with military pilots or test pilots, civilians rarely having the option of a parachute. Test pilots often have the added moral pressure of the requirement to bring the aircraft back at all costs, so that the defect, in what might well be a valuable prototype or experimental aircraft, can be more easily discovered and rectified in the future. The problem is to make a rational assessment in a tense situation without allowing bravado to overcome straightforward common sense. This is the story of Ben Gunn, the Boulton Paul test pilot who made each of the two available choices during his long and distinguished career.

Alexander Ewen Gunn, more widely known as Ben Gunn, was born on 24 June 1923 and educated in Whitehill in Glasgow. From 1942 to 1943 he attended the RAF Staff College Cranwell. He then went to No. 501 Squadron, flying Spitfires, and flying patrols over the beaches of D-Day amongst other sorties. He then moved to No. 274 Squadron, flying Tempest Mk Vs.

On VE Day he became a military test pilot at the Aeroplane and Armament Experimental Establishment at Boscombe Down. In 1947 he joined Course No. 7 at the Empire Test Pilots' School at RAE Farnborough. Following graduation he became heavily involved with the test-flying of the rivals for the RAF's new advanced trainer order, the Avro Athena and the Boulton Paul Balliol.

After both of Boulton Paul's test pilots, Robin Lindsay Neale and Peter Tisshaw, were killed in 1948, test-flying a Balliol at Wolverhampton, Ben was seconded to the company to continue the programme. He liked the variety of aircraft he saw in the flight sheds at Wolverhampton. Apart from the Balliol prototypes there was a Fairey Spearfish, having a de-icing rig; fitted, Wellingtons being overhauled and converted to navigation trainers; Hornets having target-towing gear fitted; a Lancaster with a gust-alleviation system; and 'behind the black curtains' the first of two experimental delta wing jets under construction.

When JD North, the managing director of Boulton Paul, asked him if he wanted to become the company's new chief test pilot, he said he would, but did not think the RAF would release him. One phone call from North and twenty-four hours later Ben was a civilian once more.

The delta wing jets under construction, the P111 and the P120, were in response to Specifications E.27/46 and E.27/49, as part of a Government-funded research programme into delta wing aircraft. The two aircraft were fundamentally similar, both being diminutive aircraft powered by a single Rolls-Royce Nene of 5100 lb st. The P111, which was ready first, was a pure delta with no tailplane but alternative wing tips of varying shape, and a tall triangular fin. Ben Gunn undertook taxiing trials on the grass runway at Wolverhampton, after which it was decided to change the nosewheel to a double-surface carrier type, but the first flight was made by Squadron Leader Smyth of the RAE Aero Flight at Boscombe Down.

Ben soon became involved in the test-flying of the little delta and found it hypersensitive. It had a theoretical rate of roll of 560 degrees/sec at 500 knots, which was ridiculous. A movement of the control column one inch to the side and back was enough to induce a complete roll. The problem was the early power-assisted controls that Boulton Paul had designed for the aircraft. Those early prototype PCUs suffered both by being too sensitive, and having no feedback to the pilot.

After the P111 suffered a wheels-up landing on 29 August 1952 and was returned to the company for repair, the opportunity to install a variable 'feel' system was taken. This meant that overly large movements of the controls could not be made, and the 'flying on a knife-edge' feeling was abated.

72. **Ben Gunn in the cockpit o
the P111 delta, outside the
Boulton Paul flight sheds.**

The second delta, the P120, was fitted with a swept fin, and had a delta all-moving tailplane, which operated as a trimming surface activated by a separate button on the control column. The pointed wing tips were moveable, for lateral and pitch trimming operated by further switches, on the port side console.

The P120 was moved to Boscombe Down for its first flight at the end of August 1952, which Ben was to make this time. Because of the aircraft's high take-off speed it was not possible to undertake straight hops, the test-pilot's confidence booster, but having flown the very similar P111 he did not expect any problems. His confidence was to prove misplaced.

The speed built up quickly after he released the brakes, but 20 seconds later Ben was exceedingly worried. After three quarters of the very long runway had been consumed, with the pungent smell of burning rubber seeping into the cockpit, and 175 knots indicated, the P120 was still very much stuck to the ground. Telling himself that the aircraft had been designed to fly, and fly it would, he made one last effort to haul it into the air.

With only a minimal amount of runway left, the P120 wallowed and staggered into the air, flashing right over the heads of some startled potato pickers just beyond the airfield. With the slowest rate of climb he had ever experienced, Ben decided to leave the undercarriage down and to make a wide circuit. It was clear that the all-moving tailplane had been set at the wrong angle for take-off. By trial and error, using the sliding button set on the control column, he adjusted the angle until the aircraft was flying more comfortably.

He still feared that the aircraft had a burst tyre. It was therefore essential that he make as smooth a landing as possible, even though he had to literally fly the aircraft onto the ground, though having adjusted the tailplane this was accomplished at a speed 40 knots less than that at which he had taken off. He was lucky, and although the nosewheel was badly damaged it had remained inflated, and the P120 was brought to a halt with the aid of the tail parachute.

As Ben said later, "If one believed the old sailor's tale about bad launchings. . . it was certainly true of this aeroplane"

After the inauspicious first flight, tests of the P120 went very well. The flight speed was raised in increments of 15 knots, and he found the aircraft handled pleasantly. It was painted all-black in preparation for an appearance in to the 1952 Farnborough Air Show. Then on 28 August, after 11 hours, flying the P120 made its last flight.

The flight speed was raised to 435 knots, 'which as it turned out was five knots too many'. With the test completed, Ben was over Lee-on-Solent and was turning back towards Boscombe when there was a loud buzz followed by the loudest bang he had ever heard in an aircraft. The P120 immediately went into a series of rapid rolls to port and into a dive, which caused him great difficulty in orientating himself. He shoved the control column fully starboard, but this only slowed up the rate of roll, so he put on full starboard rudder. To his relief the rolling stopped, but the aircraft was still diving rapidly towards the ground.

73. Ben Gunn flying the P120 delta on its penultimate flight.

With the controls in their present position; the aircraft should have been violently flick-rolling to starboard. However, when he pulled back the control column to haul himself out of the dive, the little jet began rolling to port again. The pitot head was pointing up at 45 degrees and the top foot was bent backwards, so he did not know his airspeed. On this occasion the trimming tailplane was to save the situation. He pressed the operating button a degree at a time, and slowly the nose came up, until, with full nose-up trim, he was once more looking at blue sky.

He called Boscombe to seek their help in getting him down, but realised he was on his own. At least he was now regaining some altitude and had a chance to assess the situation, but he had no idea what had happened. In fact, a severe flutter had occurred in the port elevon, which had snapped all the hinges. A junior test engineer at Boulton Paul had calculated that this would happen, but his figures had not been believed. It was fortunate for Boulton Paul's reputation that the accident did not happen more publicly at Farnborough the following weekend.

'How am I going to get this down?' thought Ben as he set course for Boscombe, and gingerly began a descent. Down to about 3000 feet, he decided to jettison the canopy to prepare for all eventualities. This was in fact the only way he had of removing the canopy himself, as it was normally screwed down by the ground crew before take-off. With the canopy off he could see the trailing edge of the port wing, which was torn and tattered, and he was beginning to realise what had happened. Over the hills south of Boscombe the air was a little more bumpy, and the aircraft began slowly rolling to port once more. As he had no more control left he decided the time had come to abandon any thoughts he had of making a landing, and reached for the ejection seat face-blind.

Luckily, the spring 'feel' in the control circuit caused the control column to snap into the central, neutral position, so it did not remove his leg as he ejected, but this only helped turn the aircraft to the inverted position as he left it, ejecting downwards. As he was upside down, the seat's drogue-chute did not work properly, and he was tumbling and falling with the ground rapidly approaching. He decided to pull the rip cord, to at least try and show those who investigated that he was conscious and trying to do something, even though this was contrary to the proper drill. After pulling it, he felt his lap-strap, and ran his fingers along it and turned the buckle. Luckily, the seat parted company enough for his parachute to Roman-candle, and almost immediately he crashed through a tree.

He found himself lying on his back on the ground, with blood all over his face. A twig had ripped up his nose and pushed off his helmet. He looked around and saw the parachute rip-cord alongside him, showing how close he had been to disaster. If he had waited to pull it until after he had parted company with the seat, he would have been too near the ground. He struggled to his feet, though he had had a bad crack on the ankle and had broken his arm.

'Now we have Nemesis, Fate, whatever you like to call it,' he said recalling it years later. He hobbled down the hill to a small cottage that seemed rather familiar. On the wall inside was a calendar featuring a Boulton Paul Balliol and North American T-28 flying in formation over the Grand Canyon. It was the Boulton Paul calendar for the year 1952! He realised that it was the cottage of one of his former colleagues at Boscombe, Pinky Stark. An old gentleman inside, who had heard the crash and was calling the emergency services, asked him if he was alright and offered him a drink. Ben telephoned Boscombe first, and then thought he had better go to the toilet and check for internal injuries before he took a drink. When everything seemed alright, he sank into an armchair, and a bottle of brandy was placed alongside him. By the time the ambulance arrived there was very little left in the bottle!

In one final postscript to the tale of the P120, Boulton Paul's insurance company phoned him up shortly afterwards. They thanked him very much for saving them £750,000, which was the sum they were to cover the aircraft for from midnight the following Friday, so it could take part in the Farnborough Air Show. They asked him if there was anything he wanted. He said that as it happened there was, a shooting stick, so he could hobble about at the Air Show. They told him to buy the most expensive one he could find, and were happy to reimburse him. He therefore became the proud owner of a £750,000 shooting stick!

Ben had become the first person ever to eject from a delta-winged aircraft and only the fifth British live ejection 'for real' overall. A former colleague of Ben's, JO 'Joe' Lancaster, had actually made the first ejection 'for real' from a British aircraft. John Oliver Lancaster had served in Bomber Command until 1943, when he went through the Empire Test Pilot's Course at Boscombe Down. At the end of the War the general manager of

Boulton Paul Aircraft, Ralph Beasley, secured his release from the RAF to serve as a production test pilot with the company, specifically to test-fly the Wellingtons, which were being overhauled by Boulton Paul and converted to navigation trainers.

Joe Lancaster left Boulton Paul to join Armstrong-Whitworth and was involved in the testing of their 'Flying Wings'. On 30 May 1949 he had been flying AW52, TS363, a twin-Nene-powered Flying Wing, over Warwickshire at 5000 feet. Violent oscillations began, which continued during a rapid descent to 3000 feet. Unable to regain control, Joe had been forced to use the new Martin-Baker Mk. 1 ejection seat, which successfully removed him from the aircraft.

Six and a half years later Ben was to have a similar decision to make. This time he chose the different option, though the circumstances were not quite so fraught as Joe Lancaster's experience, or the P120's crash. From 1953 Boulton Paul became the prime contractor for all Canberra modifications, building one-off radar development aircraft and export prototypes, and undertaking modifications from the simple installation of new pieces of equipment to major alterations, including the design and production of the interdictor Canberra's bomb-bay cannon pack.

To begin with, the company used the airfield at Defford in Worcestershire, Wolverhampton's grass runways being unsuitable for Canberras. However, when Defford closed they opened their own Flight Test Centre at the former bomber OTU airfield at Seighford just west of Stafford. They had tested the runway with a Vampire, but this lifted the old tarmac off, and so they resurfaced and extended it. They also took over and refurbished the two surviving hangars and built another one.

74. Ben Gunn with one of the many Canberras he test-flew for Boulton Paul.

Ben Gunn and his assistants, George Dunworth and John Powers, undertook the majority of the flight testing of the Canberras, which were many in number, and not without incident. On one occasion Ben was taking off at Culdrose in a minelaying Canberra, with a dummy revolving bomb-bay, and provision for further mines on the wing stubs. He was first on the runway that morning and disturbed a seagull, which was warming its feet on the tarmac. It flapped into the air and was sucked through the port engine, which stopped. Ben aborted the take-off but struck arrester gear beside the end of the runway, and came to rest overhanging the main road, giving a local bus driver quite a fright.

On a fateful New Year's Day, 1959, Ben took off from Seighford in Canberra PR7 WH779. Boulton Paul had done all the camera installations for the PR3 and PR7 Canberras, as well as photo-flash development. He pressed the button to retract the undercarriage and then there was a huge bang, the sort of bang to instantly clear a Scottish test pilot's head despite it being New Year's Day. The undercarriage was only partially retracted and there had been a complete hydraulic failure.

With the help of the personnel in the tower he assessed the situation. The nosewheel and one mainwheel was up, but the other mainwheel was only partially up. With no hydraulics, Ben had no flaps so a landing would have to be at relatively high speed and a belly landing at that, with the undercarriage half down. An alternative would have been to fly to the coast, point the aircraft out to sea and eject, but he had on board a Boulton Paul technician not well versed in ejection procedures. In any case, the aircraft remained fully controllable and there was plenty of time to prepare for the landing, as he flew round and round Seighford using up as much of the fuel as he could.

Eventually he came in to land on the runway and shut off the engines immediately, skidding onto the grass and towards the hedge. Unfortunately, a large tree had been cut down in the hedge, but the stump was left. Sod's Law being what it is, the Canberra was sliding straight towards it. With the

75. Canberra PR7, WH779, on New Year's Day 1959, the result of Ben's forced landing with total hydraulic failure.

wheels up and therefore no brakes, and with the engines shut off, Ben could do nothing, except sit there and wait for the crash. Both he and the technician were unhurt, and so they adjourned to the 'Hollybush' in Seighford and celebrated the first day of 1959 in a less destructive fashion.

Ben continued test-flying for Boulton Paul until 1965, mostly Canberras of different Marks. The company also took on Lightning work from English Electric, especially the F3 development programme, but the Lightnings were flown by BAC test pilots. In 1965 the disgraceful cancellation of TSR2 had its effect on Boulton Paul, as the British Aircraft Corporation took back all the Canberra and Lightning work for its own divisions and the Flight Test Centre at Seighford was closed. Ben went to work for Rover Gas Turbines for a year, and then went to Beagle Aircraft. When that too was closed by a short-sighted Government he became manager of Shoreham Airport. He was one of that famous cadre of British test pilots from the 1950s who survived. He had lived through some of those heart-stopping in-flight bangs, which are the dread of all test pilots, and made all the right decisions, whether to bale out or try for a forced landing.

CHAPTER 22

Down in the Yukon

Arctic air travel has claimed many aircraft over the years, even famous names like Roald Amundsen. In this region navigation was as difficult as it could be, before the era of satellite navigation. There were few maps, and there were the problems of the magnetic pole and the approach to a point where every direction is south. There is also the extra hazard of appalling weather conditions, and few weather stations to predict the weather ahead. The era of the jet airliner, for the first time meant that trans-Arctic travel became routine, allowing pioneering airlines like Scandinavian Airlines System (SAS) to take the short cut from Europe to the west coast of America. For the light aircraft, however, flying in the Arctic was as dangerous as always.

In October 1967 three valiant flyers prepared to make the first trans-Arctic trip in a light aircraft, a twin-engined Piper Aztec. The route would take them from Alaska to Norway, via the northern reaches of Canada and Greenland. The three men were no amateur adventurers, they were professional aircrew with long experience of Arctic flying conditions. Though in part they were seeking the glory of being first, they were also attempting to pioneer a safe route between Alaska and Europe for light aircraft, which might become generally used in later years.

The senior pilot was to be Thor Tjontveit, an Alaskan of Norwegian descent, who was a pilot on Wien Alaska Airlines. The co-pilot was less experienced, being only 22 years old. He was Rolf Storhaug the son of an SAS captain. Finally, the navigator was 48-year old Einar Sverre Pedersen, the chief navigator of SAS, who had played an important role in pioneering the trans-Polar route ten years previously.

The aircraft was a Piper PA-23 Aztec, a widely used four to six-seat light aircraft powered by two 250 hp Lycoming O-540 engines. They named the aircraft *Spirit of Fairbanks*, though the flight would commence in Anchorage, and also painted on the side 'Anchorage – Oslo, 29 Hours. First twin-engined aircraft over the Pole.' As it turned out they had somewhat jumped the gun with this claim.

The normal range of an Aztec was 1200 miles at 200 mph cruising speed, so the flight had to be planned over several short stages, leaving plenty of reserves to reach alternative airfields if that were at all possible. From Anchorage they would go via Fairbanks to Inuvik, one of the biggest fur-trading centres in northern Canada. They would then traverse the northern reaches of Canada via the weather stations at Mould Bay, Isachsen, Eureka and Alert. They would then go via northern Greenland, to Spitzbergen and then to Tromsø in northern Norway, before heading south to Oslo. They estimated the flight would take 29 hours, including stops for refuelling.

The major concern was the navigation. Navigation aids were almost non existent in the region, and a magnetic compass was entirely useless as the magnetic pole was only 600 miles distant. There was a Loran station on the north-west Coast, but the signals from this were adversely affected by the conductivity of the permanently frozen tundra. Map-reading, the mainstay of light aircraft navigation, could not be trusted either. The only maps of the region were based on aerial photographs, and could be misleading, especially when so much of the landscape looked like an endless vista of snow-covered mountains. There are no towns or other man-made features to help identify the position on the ground, and in any case in mid-October, when they would be taking off, there were only about 5 hours of daylight in those latitudes.

The pioneering work done by the airlines that flew the route, had produced new grid maps and the Polar Path Gyro, and it was on these that Sverre Pedersen would rely on to steer their course. A forced landing was always a possibility in a light aircraft, and so the Aztec was loaded up with many days of provisions in case of this eventuality.

Having positioned themselves from Anchorage to Fairbanks for the start of the pioneering part of the flight, they took off for Inuvik on Friday 13 October, an inauspicious date on which to start. The Aztec was fully fuelled and heavily laden, and it was already afternoon when they set course for Fort Yukon on the Yukon River. Before long, darkness fell and the long hours of the Arctic night fell over the landscape. The shortness of the day meant they intended to complete most of the journey during the hours of darkness.

As they crossed the Canadian border in the early hours of 14 October, the flight had been uneventful. At about 3 am they flew over the small town of Old Crow, on the Porcupine River, at a height of 9500 feet. They reported their position over the radio, and this was acknowledged. Just after this the port engine began to run rough, and shortly afterwards stopped completely.

They considered the options, and agreed to continue on to Inuvik, which was about 170 miles from Old Crow. There was no reason to think that the other engine would let them down. They thought the fuel pump on the port engine had packed up. With a much reduced fuel load, they should be able to make it on one engine. The most serious problem, however, was that the port engine ran the dynamo, which powered the electrical system, so that the radio no longer worked, and they could not report their situation. Not only that, the gyro and other powered instruments no longer worked, and neither did the lights.

It soon became clear, however, that they were unable to maintain height on the power of the starboard engine alone. A forced landing looked inevitable, but all they could see below them was the Richardson Mountains, which reached up to over 5600 feet. A forced landing there would mean almost certain death. They decided to alter course to the north, where there was lower ground. They aimed in the general direction of a radar station at Shingle Point, where there was a small airstrip. They reasoned that even if they could not make the strip, the radar station might pick them up on their screens and then notice when they went down.

They had not been flying on their new course for more then five minutes when the starboard engine began spluttering, and then shortly afterwards it too stopped. They quickly searched the mountain landscape in the semi-darkness below. Luckily, they could see an opening in the mountains, which sloped gently downwards in their direction of flight. Tjontveit aimed for this slope as they all tightened their straps and braced themselves for the landing.

They came in to land at about 80 mph, and hit the ground with a resounding crash. The Aztec careered down the slope, the outer wings snapping off outboard of the engines. Inside the three men were banged around, but luckily they did not run over or hit anything very large. Eventually, the Aztec slid sideways and then came to a halt. The fuselage was still intact, and luckily it did not burst into flames.

Once they had regained their senses, with the relief of still being alive, and not badly hurt, they examined their situation. Pedersen was the most badly hurt. He had clearly broken his arm, and also had cuts and grazes to his head and face. Tjontveit had receive a heavy blow on the back of his head and Storhaug had a black eye and a bruised foot. They set about methodically dressing their various injuries, with torn strips of cloth.

They assessed their situation, deciding to follow the first rule of Arctic survival and stay with the wrecked aircraft. They knew an air search would be initiated for them when they became overdue at Inuvik, and the easiest thing for the rescuers to spot would be the aircraft. They had two or three weeks' of supplies, so there was no problem on that score. Their greatest problem was going to be the cold, with night-time temperatures routinely dropping to minus 15 or 20 degrees Centigrade. The interior of the wrecked aircraft did not provide much shelter, so they began a search of the valley for something better.

They noticed both rabbits and ptarmigans in the valley, which would supplement their food supply if they were there for any length of time. They had not gone beyond the treeline that stretched through the region, so there was wood to make a fire. Eventually, they set up camp about a mile from the wreck in a sheltered spot where they could keep a fire going. They hoped the smoke from the fire would help searching planes to find them.

When they went down, the disappearance had been noticed on radar screens, and a rescue centre was established at Elmendorf Air Force Base near Anchorage. The searchers faced a daunting task, co-ordinating both American and Canadian searchers over an area roughly the size of Sweden. The air search from Inuvik was led by Flight Lieutenant John Crowford of the Royal Canadian Air Force and involved up to ten military and civil aircraft.

Mrs Pedersen flew from Sweden with her 20 year-old son Sverre. On their arrival in Anchorage, they heard that a man had been spotted by one of the searching aircraft, standing next to a fire. Her hopes were quickly

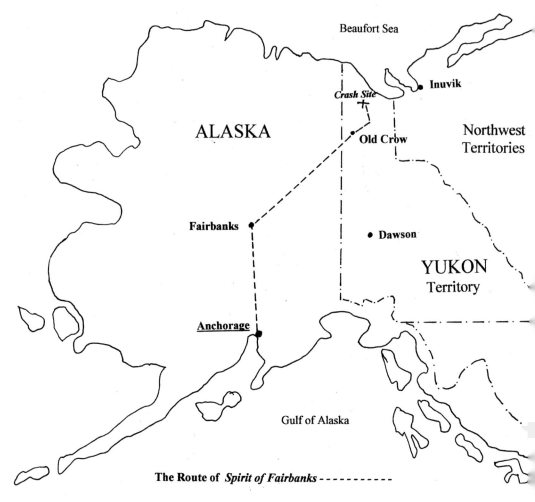

76 The route of the final flight of *Spirit of Fairbanks*.

dashed when the pilot reported that the man was clearly a hunter. Mrs Pedersen was allowed to board some of the searching aircraft to take part in the search herself.

Soon after the hunter was sighted the weather took a turn for the worse, with strong winds and snow, hampering the rescuers. The three downed men huddled in their makeshift shelter as the blizzard raged around them. They knew they could survive, even in those conditions, for some time. They were already rationing their food, because they knew they had been off course, which would mean the search would take longer than if they had stuck to their planned track.

During the first week they heard the sound of aero engines twice. They actually saw a DC-3 droning by and frantically waved and signalled with a mirror to attract the attention of the crew. They threw petrol on the fire and sent sheets of flame shooting into the air, but it was to no avail. They were not seen.

After nine days in the frozen wilderness they were spotted not by the systematic searching but by sheer coincidence. A Fokker Friendship, flown by Robert Shinn with Ronald Wood as co-pilot, was forced to take a more northern track by bad weather, just as they had done. This took the Friendship over an area that had not been searched, and as they scanned the ground below, Shinn suddenly noticed the wrecked Piper.

As Shinn brought the airliner round for a second low pass over the wreck, they noticed the three men frantically waving by their shelter a little way away. Knowing they would shortly be rescued, the men gave up their rationing system, and hungrily devoured their food. The following day a rescue team reached them, and after ten days in the Arctic wilderness they were taken out.

They had been extremely lucky. The forced landing had been reasonably successful; they had survived with only minor injuries, when they could so easily have been killed; and they were found by an aircraft that should not have been where it was. The decision had just been made to search more to the east, well away from where they had forced landed. Who knows what would have happened to them, if Robert Shinn had not been forced off course, and over their lonely camp.

CHAPTER 23

Down in the Oman

Many of the stories in this book have described aircraft coming down in out of the way places and the subsequent search for them, with the searchers often having scant knowledge of their exact whereabouts. This final chapter is slightly different as it describes my own search for a downed aircraft, a Vickers Valetta, in the arid mountains of Oman, though the aircraft had come down many years before.

I arrived in the Sultanate of Oman in late 1977 to work for George Wimpey & Co. on the construction of a huge police training complex at a barren site about 20 kilometres from Nizwa. This town lies on the western side of the Hajar Mountains, about 150 kilometres from Muscat on the coast. Before I left for Oman I bought a book about the country, and was intrigued by a sentence in it which read 'On the approach to Nizwa Airport we saw the shell of an aircraft which crashed in 1958'. I resolved to look for this wreck as soon as an opportunity presented itself, and to find out what had caused it to come down.

I quickly discovered that 'Nizwa Airport' was just a gravel strip in the desert next to the village of Firq, with a few fuel drums next to a barasti (palm leaf) shelter. It was right alongside Wimpey's gravel-crushing plant in the wadi, which ran parallel. As one of my duties included checking on the output of the plant each day, I was able to keep a close eye on what was a surprisingly active runway. On top of the Hajar Mountains, 6000 feet up, was the Jebel Akhdar (Green Mountain), a plateau of agricultural land

77. The wreckage of Valetta, VW817, by the airstrip at Firq.

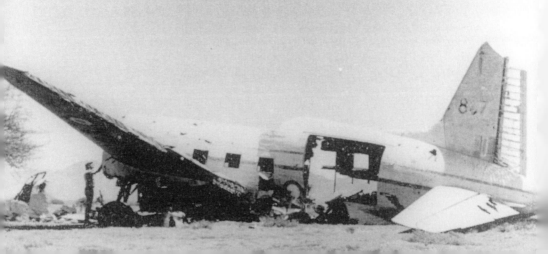

round the village of Saiq. The only way up there was by donkey path or to a short airstrip that had been built by the British. The Sultan of Oman's Air Force (SOAF) ran a shuttle service up there from Firq airstrip, mostly using Short Skyvans, but occasionally with Bell UH-1 helicopters and Britten-Norman Islanders.

I watched them landing and taking off almost every day, as well as other occasional visitors like Taylor-Woodrow's Twin Otter. What I could not see anywhere around the airstrip was any sign of a wrecked aircraft. Enquiries led me to discover that there were two other airstrips near to Nizwa, one by the wadi on the other side of the town, and one next to the army barracks.

Nizwa is one of the largest towns in the Oman, hidden mostly underneath a large grove of date palms, but with the souk (market), mosque and a large stone fort in the centre. During the Imam's revolt against the rule of the Sultan, in the late 1950s, this fort had been rocketed by British Venoms, as part of the military assistance the British gave the Sultan in quelling the revolt.

The old Sultan had been greatly against western influence creeping into Omani society. As late as 1970, despite being the second largest country on the Arabian peninisula, Oman possessed only 10 kilometres of tarmac road, and fewer than 1000 Omani children went to school. The old Sultan was removed almost bloodlessly by his son, Sultan Qaboos bin Sa'id, with the help of the British, and since then huge strides have been made in modernising the country.

An investigation of the airstrip beyond Nizwa, revealed that it was long disused. There was very little open area around, in an area where a wadi ran alongside the mountains from the village of Tanuf to Nizwa. Tanuf was completely deserted, and in ruins. As part of the suppression of the Imam's revolt the people of Tanuf had been ordered out of their village, and it was then blown up by the British Army.

The last airstrip was by the army barracks, then occupied by the Jebel Regiment. A quick look at this short strip told me that there were no aircraft wrecks around it. Not only was it very short, but at one end was the army camp and at the other there was a 800 foot cliff, which meant taking off and landing were always done in the same direction. The only aircraft I ever saw use this strip, apart from helicopters, were the Pilatus Turbo-Porters of the Oman Police, though I have been assured that both Skyvans and Caribous, with heavy loads have also used this strip.

The police operated a sizeable air force of their own, and several of their Jet Ranger and Bell UH-1 helicopters were frequent visitors to our site, as it was a police training centre. They even operated a BAC 111 airliner, mainly for communications with Salalah, the southern part of Oman, separated from the north by the tail end of the Empty Quarter.

It was clear that the wreck mentioned in the book had to be in sight of the approach to the strip at Firq, but this could include many square miles of desert. The ground looked flat before you started to cross it, but was in fact very broken, criss-crossed with wadis and various hollows, any of which could have hidden the wreck.

Our day off was Friday, and during most Fridays I borrowed a Suzuki

Jeep, or if I was lucky a Land Rover, and set out to explore this area, in as systematic a way as I could. I started with the area beneath the approach taken by the SOAF Skyvans when they flew up to Firq from Seeb Airport on the coast. The going was very slow indeed. Every hundred yards or so, I would find myself on the edge of a wadi into which I would have to find a way to drive down, and then another way to drive out. The temperature was usually around 100°F in the shade, and there was no shade. Even the jeeps I usually used were open-topped. On some days in the height of the summer it reached 120°F, within half a degree of 50°C.

There was no sign of the wreck, and my frustration increased. Then my attention was diverted by tales of other wrecks in the area. I was told of one at Ibri airstrip, to the north of Nizwa. One Friday I took a Land Rover and barrelled up the gravel road through Bahla to Ibri. There turned out to be two strips at Ibri. I passed the larger one before reaching the town. There was an American registered Turbo-Commander parked on it, by the road. It was quite strange to find an expensive aircraft parked in the desert with nothing in sight for miles in any direction, except arid scrub and rocky jebels.

The wreck was by the smaller strip right next to the town. At the approach to the strip was the forward fuselage and engine of a Scottish Aviation Pioneer CC1. On the slope beyond the strip were the wings and tail-cone, peppered with bullet holes. I later found out that the aircraft was XL554, a Pioneer operated by SOAF, which had turned over in a crosswind landing on 14 April 1960. The bullet holes were because the strip was next to an army firing range, and the aircraft was useful for target practice. In fact, most Omani men in the mountains habitually carry rifles, usually Lee-Enfields, so it's not unusual to find bullet holes in anything convenient for a bit of target practice.

When the Sultan's Air Force was formed in 1959, Pioneer CC1 XL554 was one of the first two aircraft taken on charge, together with another ex-No. 78 Squadron Pioneer, XL518, having been previously based at Khormaksar, Aden. These two aircraft were soon joined by three Percival Provost T52s as the armed element of SOAF for anti-guerrilla operations. The Ibri strip was just one of seventy-eight desert airstrips scattered throughout the Sultanate.

Discovering this wreck fired up my enthusiasm again, and the following Friday I set out to search once more for the wreck near Nizwa. I searched another huge chunk of desert, up to five miles from the Firq airstrip, but once more found nothing.

In my investigations into the Pioneer wreck I discovered that there was another Pioneer wreck by an airstrip at the village of Awabi, which was on the other side of the Hajar Mountains near the town of Rostaq. On a day long expedition there I had little difficulty finding the strip, though I could see why Pioneers were the aircraft operated from it. It was disused and seemed little longer than the football pitch that was marked out on one end of it. I was amazed when I later heard from a SOAF pilot that he once took a Skyvan into this strip. Despite the fact that the aircraft was empty, he said the subsequent take-off was 'interesting to say the least'.

78. The forward fuselage of Pioneer XL554 by the airstrip at Ibri.

One thing was certain, there was no sign of a Pioneer wreck anywhere around the strip, though I later discovered the aircraft had been XL701, an RAF aircraft not SOAF, which had crashed there during a night landing. As the strip was surrounded on three sides by mountains, I was not surprised to hear this.

The SAS men who sometimes came down out of the mountains for a bit of R and R at our camp informed me that there was a well-known de Havilland Venom wreck near the village of Saiq. The aircraft had been attacking rebels in the area *circa* 1960, and had either been hit by ground fire or the pilot had failed to pull out. Armed with exact instructions about how to find one of the paths up to the plateau from near the village of Iski, I set out one Friday and got lost. After struggling for 3000 feet up the mountains I was faced with a sheer cliff, and decided to forget all about the Venom wreck.

The following week I returned to the search for the Nizwa wreck; at least I could look for that in a jeep. One Friday I finally came to the conclusion that I was never going to find it. I was standing on the bonnet of my jeep in the centre of the 25 square miles of desert that I estimated I had searched, scanning the horizon. There was nothing to be seen except rocks and scrub vegetation. I gave up and headed back to camp. When I got back to the camp road I cast one last glance towards the airstrip a hundred yards away, and noticed for the first time, something large and black lying under a stunted tree. I thought it must be an abandoned oil drum, but drove over to investigate. It was a large aircraft wheel and tyre, still attached to an undercarriage leg. Lying next to it was an almost undamaged four-blade propeller!

All around were small bits of aircraft wreckage, but the only other substantial piece was part of the frame of a door. I had found the site of the wreck, but most of the wreckage must have been taken away in the previous two years. I had driven within sight of the wheel every day for the last six months and had not seen it. The wheel clearly came from a multi-engined aircraft and the door frame displayed the white upper fuselage and blue cheatline of an RAF Transport Command aircraft. The four-blade propeller led me to think it must have been a Vickers Valetta.

After I had convinced the disbelieving drinkers in Wimpey's bar that I had found an aircraft propeller lying in the desert, a party of volunteers arranged to bring it back to camp. It was then cleaned up, painted, and hung on the wall of Wimpey's site club, which was later turned over to the Oman police as part of their training complex. As far as I know it is still there. All that remained was to research how the aircraft came to be at Nizwa.

Vickers Valetta VW817 was one of three Valettas on detachment with No.78 Squadron at Bahrain in 1958–9. No. 78 Squadron was basically a Twin Pioneer squadron operating throughout the Gulf and in Southern Arabia. The Valettas were used on a regular supply run. In January 1959 VW817 was flown to Firq with No. 78 Squadron personnel on board. As it landed the starboard mainwheel tyre burst. This caused the aircraft to slew round, and to rear up on its nose. As the nose hit the desert it caused the aircraft to crash back onto its tail, breaking the fuselage just behind the wings.

Everyone evacuated the aircraft as quickly as they could and examined the wreck, which was clearly a write-off. Another 78 Squadron Valetta landed at Firq a week later, having to land over the wreck, which was still on the strip. They salvaged what they could from VW817, including the engines, and the rest was then towed off the runway by an army recovery vehicle. There it lay for nearly twenty years until the carcass was finally cleared away, leaving just a few fragments for me to discover – a reminder of those heart-stopping moments for the crew and passengers of VW817, all those years before; their own moment of one per cent blind panic.

79. The Valetta's prop being transported to the Wimpey club for preservation.

INDEX

Page numbers in *italics* refer to illustrations

Achatina 56
Adams, Billy 92
Adams, S.Sgt Samuel 117, 121
airship N1 (*Norge*) 37-39
Airspeed Oxford 140, 141-142, *142*, 145
Alcock, Captain John 50
Alda, Captain Julio Ruiz de 51-52
Alexandria 72
Allen, Damar Leslie 14-15
America, first flight from Australia to 67
Amundsen, Roald 34, *34*, 35, 36, 37, 38, 39, 42, *43*, 44, 45, 59
Anderson, Keith 59, 60, 64, 66
Andrews, LAC 76
Anglesey 11-12, 15-16, 17
Anson, Major CR 74, 79
Arctic, the 34, 35-36, 38-39, 122, 123, 125-126, 163-167, *166 see also* North Pole
Armitage, Flight Lieutenant Jack 128, 129-131
Armstrong Whitworth
AW52 Flying Wing 160
Awana 47
Siskin II/III 47
Whitley 92-93, *94*, 95, *95*, 96, 98, 99-101
Wolf 47
Arrow Active 109
Asinara Island 130
Assiut, Egypt 23
Atlantic Ferry Organisation (ATFERO) 113, 122
Atlantic Ocean 9
  attempts at flights across 47-48, 50, 51, 52, 54-56
  ditchings/forced landings in 51-52, 55-56, 113, 122, 123, 125-126
Australia and England, flights between 61, 63-66, 67, 68, 74-75, *75*, 78-82, *79*, *82*, *83*
Australia to America, first flight from 67
Australian National Airways Ltd 61, 66, 67
Australian outback, forced landings in 58, 63-66, *65*
Avery, Sergeant PH 100-101
Avro Avian 67
Avro Lancaster 132, 133, 134-137, 139, *139*
Avro Ten 61, 67
Awabi, Oman 170, 171
Azores, Horta harbour 54

Backhouse, Pilot Officer R 128, 129-131
Bardon, Flight Lieutenant HR 76
Barnett, Flight Sergeant NW 128, 129-131
Barwell, Eric 84, *84*, 85-86, 87, *87*, 88, 89-90, 91, *91*
Barwell, Wing Commander Phillip 85
Beardmore Inflexible 73
Beasley, Ralph 159-160
Beaulieu 9
Behaeghe, Lieutenant 28, 31, 32
Beires, Sarmento 52
Belgian Air Force 28-29, 31, 32, 33
Belgian Army 29, 33
Bennett, Floyd 37
Bennett, JM 59
Berlin raid 93, 95
Black Country, forced landings in 108, 109-111, *111*
Blackburn Beverley 82-83
Blackburn Roc *147*, 148
Blackpool, Squires Gate aerodrome 149
Blackpool Meeting (1910) 10
Blériot, Louis, and flying schools 9, 14
Blériot Monoplane 14-16, *15*, 18, *19*, 20
bomb, 12,000 lb Tallboy 132, 135, 138
Bombay-to-Baroda railway line 20

Borges, Larre 52
Boscombe Down 157, 158
Boulton Paul Aircraft Ltd 47, 147-148, *148*, 149, 154, 155, 156, 158, 160, 162
Balliol 149-150, 152, *152*, *153*, 154, 155
Bolton *48*
Bugle 47
Defiant 84-88, *87*, 89-90, 91, *91*
Defiant Mark I 91, 102, 103, 104-105, 106-107, *106*, *107*, 148-149
Defiant Mark II 148, 149
Overstrand 149
P3 Bobolink 47
P7 Bourges 47, 48
P8 Atlantic 47-48, *49*, 50, 51
P111 156, *156*
P120 156, 157-159, *158*
Boulton Paul Association 91, 105-107, *107*
Bournemouth Flying Meeting (1910) 9-10
Bradshaw, Granville Eastwood 18, 19
Brain, Lester 66
Brazy, Gilbert 42
Brew, Alec 168, 169-172
Brisbane, Eagle Farm Airport 68
Briscoe, Wing Commander A 76
Bristol Tourer 59, 60
British Aircraft Corporation TSR2 162
Brown, Lieutenant Arthur Whitten 50
Browne, Cecil 50
Bueger, Commandant de 28, 31, 33
Bunkell, Slim 149
Burr, Admiral 13
Byrd, Richard Evelyn 37, 38

Calloway, Group Captain W 76
Camel Corps, Imperial 23, 24
Cannock Chase 111-112
Cape Town, record flights between London and 109
Carey, Flying Officer Daniel William 'Bill', DFC 133, 134-135, 136-139
Castiau, Lieutenant 28, 33
Castilho, Jorge de 52
Cedric 56
Chantier 38
Charcot, Dr 36
Charlton Athletic Football Club 141, 145
Chunn, Sergeant 102, 103
City of Milan 39, 42
Cleere, Sergeant 93, *95*
Coffman, Captain Robert E 122, 123, 125-126, *126*
Colignon, Lieutenant 29, 32
Columbus 56
Comper Swift 108
Compton, Colonel Keith 117
Congo, River 27, 28, 29
Consolidated B-24 Liberator 118, 122-123
  B-24D *Lady be Good* 117, 118-120, *119*, 121
Cooke, Flight Lieutenant Nicholas 85
Corbett-Wilson, D 14-15, *14*, 16-17
Courtney, Captain Frank 46-47, 48, *48*, 50, 52, *53*, 54-56, 57
Craig, Pilot Officer James 103, 104, *104*, 105, 145
Crichton, Flight Lieutenant David 'Doc', MBE 144
Crocombe, Fred F 73, *75*, 78-79, 81-82, 83
Croker, Edgar Alfred 'Ted' 140, *140*, 141, 142-144, 145-146, *146*
Crossio, Lieutenant V 51
Crowell, Major John 126
Crowford, Flight Lieutenant John 165
Culverwell, Sergeant 96

Cuverville, Lieutenant Cavelier de 42

Dale, WOG 128, 129-131
Dart Aircraft Ltd 147
Darwin W/T station 80, 81, 82
Davies (ground engineer) 74, 78, 81
Dawes, Captain George William Patrick 18, 19-21, *19*
de Havilland DH66 Hercules 64-65, 67
de Havilland Leopard Moth 108, 109
de Havilland Venom 171
de Havilland Canada Chipmunk *146*
Dietrichson, Lief 35, 36, 44
Dornier Wal 34, 35, 36, 46, 50-52, *51, 53,* 54-57, *55, 56*
Douglas Boston 113, *114,* 115
Douglas C-47 118-119, *119*
Douglas World Cruiser 51
Dowthwaite, Flying Officer John 141, 142-143, 144, 146
Drake, Pilot Officer 96
Drysdale Mission, Australia 63
Dublin, Phoenix Park 16
Dunkirk 84, 86-87, 88, 89, 96
Dunn, Wing Commander WH 71, 72
Dunstall Park, Wolverhampton, and Meeting 9, 18-19, *19,* 20
Dunworth, George 161
Dyk, Evert van 66

Ellsworth, Lincoln 34-35, 37, 38
Endean, Jack 152
England, Eric Gordon 73-74
England and Australia, flights between 61, 63-66, 67, 68, 74-75, *75,*
    78-82, *79, 82, 83*
English Channel 9, 16, 84, 89-90
English Electric Canberra 160, *160,* 161, 162
    Canberra PR7 161-162, *161*

Farley, Wing Commander WJ 97, 98
Farman biplane 9-11, 12, 13-14
Farnborough 46, 47
Farnes, Pilot Officer Eric 102, 103
Fawke, Squadron Leader Gerry 134
Feather, Cecil 148, 149
Felixstowe 69, *70,* 71
Feucht, Carl 35, 36
Fifi 31
Firq, Oman 168, *168,* 169, 172
Fokker
    F.VII 59, 60
    F.VIIB/3m 59, 60, 61, 73
    FK31 47
    Friendship 167
    Monoplane 37, 38 *see also Southern Cross*
Foryd aerodrome, nr Abergele 14
Fothergill, Pilot Officer C 76-77, 78
Fram 36
Franco, Ramon 51
Franks, Flight Sergeant Les 134, 135, 136-137

Gardiner (pilot) 23-24
Garside, JA 23-26
Gatchina, Russia 37
General Aircraft Monospar ST-4/ST-6 73
General Aircraft Monospar ST-10 Croydon 74-75, 75, 78-82,
    79, 82
General Aircraft Universal Freighter 82-83
George A Bond & Co. Hosiery 59
Gilmour, Hugh 52, 54, 55, 56
Gilroy (wireless operator) 74, 78, 80, 81
Glenelg, River 63, 64
Godfrey, Pilot Officer 96
Gold, Sergeant 98
Goodlet, Pilot Officer David 113, 115-116
Goose Bay, Labrador 113
Gottwaldt, Captain Birger 38
Gouveia, Manuel 52
Graf von Goetzen 27, 31, 32, 33

Grahame-White, Claude, and School 46
Greenaway, Flying Officer Norman E 122, 123, 125-126, *126*
Greenland, forced landing in 113, 115-116
Grey, George 64
Grimsby 96
Guildad, Captaine de Corvette Rene 42
Gunn, Alexander Ewen 'Ben' 155-156, *156,* 157-159, *160,*
    161-162

Hacking, Pilot Officer 95
Hamilton, Flight Lieutenant 136
Hancock, Captain Allan 60
Handasyde Monoplane 47
Handley Page Halifax 98, 100, 127, 128-130, *129*
Handley Page Hampden 122, 123, *124,* 125
Handley Page HP42 Horsa 75-77, *77,* 78
Hardy, Squadron Leader Stephen 85
Hatton, Flight Lieutenant William J 117, 118, 119-120
Hawker, Harry 50
Hawker Duiker 47
Hays, Second Lieutenant DP 117, 121
Hedwig von Wisman 27, 31
Heimdal 36, 38
Hempstead, LAC George 104, 105, 145
Hendon 14, 16, 46
Henshaw, Alex 108-112
Hever Castle, ornamental lake 71-72
Hewitt, Vivian 14, 15-16, *15,* 17
Hickman, Pilot Officer *87,* 88
Hill, Bert 103
Hill, John 103
Hill, Flight Lieutenant 69, 71
Hitchcock, Bob 59, 60, 64, 66
Hobby 36
Holden, Captain 65
Holder, N 18, 19
Horgen, First Lieutenant Emil 38
Hosmer, Elwood 52, 55, 57
Howarth, Captain AL 48
Howells, Sergeant 93, 95, *95,* 96
Humber Monoplane 18, 19
Hunter, Squadron Leader Phillip 85, 86, *87,* 88

Ibara, Captain 52
Ibri, Oman 170, *171*
Imperial Airways 72, 75-76, 78
Interstate Flying Services 59
Irish Sea 9, 10, 11, 12-17, 108
Italia airship and crew 39, *40,* 41-42, 44-45

Jebel Akhdar plateau, Oman 168-169
Jenkins, Sergeant 96
Johnson, LAC 88
'Jones, Robert' *see* Loraine, Robert
Jones, LAC 87

Kalémié (*formerly Lukuga, Albertville*) 27, 28, 29
Kigoma 27-28, 31, 32, 33
King's Bay, Svalbard 35, 36, 37-38, 39, *40,* 44
King's Cup Air Races 47, 108, 109
Kingani 28, 31
Kingsford-Smith, Charles (*later* Sir Charles) 58-59, *58,* 60-61,
    63-64, 65-66, 67-68
Kingsford-Smith, Pilot Officer 98
Koepang, Timor 80, 81, 82
Konigsberg 27
Krassin 44, *44,* 45

La Bocca, France, raid on 127-128, 131
Laconia 28
Lake Stora Lutevatten 134, 136, 138
Lake Tanganyika 27-28, 29, 31, 32-33
Lake Tongwe 29, 28-29, 31, *31,* 33
Lamotte, T.Sgt Robert 117, 121
Lancaster, Flight Lieutenant John Oliver 'Joe' 154, 159-160

Lankester Parker, John 71-72
Lapland, forced landing in 132, 136-138
Latham, Hubert 16, 84
Latham 47: 42, *43*, 44
Le Havre raid 96
Lewis, Corporal 71
Libyan Desert 22, 23-26, 118-121
Lindsay Neale, Jenny 150, 151
Lindsay Neale, Robin 147-150, *147*, *148*, 151-152, *153*, 154, 155
   sister-in-law Hazel 150, 151
Lindsay Neale, Rosemary 149, 150, 151
Liner Concrete 146
Litchfield, HA 61, 63-64, 65-66
Llandudno golf course 10-11, *10*
Locatelli, Lieutenant Antonio 51
Locker, Pilot Officer W 76
Lockheed Altair 67, 68
London and Cape Town, record flights between 109
Loraine, Robert ('Robert Jones') 9-11, *10*, 12-14, *12*, 16, 17
Loudon, Flight Lieutenant MJ 103
Lukuga (*formerly* Albertville, *now* Kalémié) 27, 28, 29
Lundberg (Swedish pilot) *42*, 44-45
Lyon, Harry 60-61

M'Toa 29, *29*, 30, 31, 32
Malcolm, HMS 90
Malmgren, Finn 38, 39, 42
Malyguin 44
Marescalchi, Lieutenant C 51
Mariano (*Italia* crewman) *42*, 45
Martinsyde Raymor 50
Martinsyde S1 Scout 46
Maud 34
McKie, Pilot Officer Alex 133, 136, 137, 138
McLennan, Pilot Officer Doug 133, 134, 135, 137, 139
McWilliams, TH 61, 63-64, 65-66
Mediterranean Sea, ditching in 128-131
Meheriq, Egypt 23, 24
Melrose, Jim 108
Midland Aero Club 18
Miles Aircraft Company 151, *151*
   Magister 92
   Messenger 150-151, *150*, *151*
Mimi 28, 31
Minnewaska, SS 56, *56*
Moir, SJ 66
Monospar Wing Company, and ST-3 73
Moore, S.Sgt Vernon 117, 121
Morgan, Pilot Officer JH 128, 129
Mussolini, Benito 37, 39, 42

Naples airfields raid 117-118
Nash, Pilot Officer Alfred 113, 115-116
Netta 28
Nimoda, SS 81
Nizwa, Oman 168, 169, 171, 172
Nobile, General Umberto 37, 38, 39, 41, 42, 44, 45
Norge airship 37-39
North, JD 46, 47, *48*, 155, 156
North Atlantic ferrying operation *see* Atlantic Ferry Organisation;
   Return Ferry Service; Royal Air Force, Transport Command
North Pole 34, 35, 37-39, *40*, 41-42, 44-45 *see also* Arctic, the
North Sea, ditchings in 92, 95-96
Northland 116
Norwich, Mousehold Aerodrome *48*, *49*, 50

Oman, Sultan of, and Air Force 169, 170
Oman, Sultanate of 168-172
Oman Police 169, 172
Omdahl, Oskar 35, 36, 38
Openshaw, Pilot Officer 93, 95, *95*
Operations, Special Duties 98, 99-100
Orta, Lieutenant 28, 31, 32, 33
Owen, HC 66
Owen, Flight Sergeant John 'Jack' 92, 93, 95, *95*, 96-97, 98-101

Pacific Ocean, first to fly across 59, 60-61
Peak District, crashes in
   Bleaklow Moor 104-105, 106, *106*, 107
   Brown Knoll 140, 142-145, *142*, *145*, 146
Pedersen, Einar Sverre 163-165, 166-167
Pedersen, Mrs 165-166
Penrhos Park 12, 13, 16
Percival Gull 67
Percival Mew Gull 109
Pethybridge, Thomas 68
Petrie-Andrews, Pilot Officer JR 127, 128, 129-131, 138
Pickett, Sergeant 96
Pierce, Fred 52, 55, 56
Piper PA-23 Aztec 163-165, *166*
Polar Bjorn, The 126
Porjus 136, 138, 139
Portugal, Dovalle 52
Pourquoi Pas 36
Powers, John 161
Pulham 37
Purvis, Pilot Officer 95

Qantas 66, 67
Qatar Peninsula, Salwah Wells 76-77, 78
Quill, Jeffrey 109

Rada, Pablo 51-52
Raleigh, USS 51
Ramm, Fredrik 38
Read, Commander 9
Return Ferry Service 122-123
Rhyl Urban District Council 16
Richmond, USS 51
Ridley, Second Lieutenant Stewart Gordon 22, 23-26
Riiser-Larsen, Hjalmar 35, 36, 37, 38, 44
Ripslinger, T.Sgt Harold 'Rip' 117, 121
Rissili, Lieutenant 51
Robertson, Bob 103-104
Robinson, Warrant Officer George 'Robbie' 141, 142-143,
   144-145, 146
Rochford, Sergeant 93
Rock, Flight Sergeant WG 100, *100*, *101*
Rolls, Charles 10
Rolls-Royce Merlin engine 110-111, 112
Royal Air Force *see also* Royal Flying Corps; Royal Naval Air Service
   No. 10 Operational Training Unit 92
   No. 11 Service Flying Training School 92
   No. 21 (Pilots) Advanced Flying Unit 140-142
   No. 45 Group 122
   Pathfinder Force 127, 131
   squadrons
      No. 4: 92
      No. 9: 132
      No. 10: 93, *94*, 95, *95*, 96
      No. 35: 127, 131
      No. 70: 76, 133-134
      No. 78: 172
      No. 84: 76
      No. 125 (Newfoundland) 91, *91*
      No. 138 (Special Duties) 97, 98-100
      No. 141: 102, 103
      No. 151: 102, 103
      No. 209: 69, 71, 72
      No. 230: 69, 71, 72
      No. 255: 102, 103-104
      No. 256: 102
      No. 264 (Madras Presidency) 84, 85-89, *86*, *87*, 91, 102
      No. 266: 85, 103
      No. 617: 132, 133, 134-136, 138
   stations
      Cosford 109, 110
      Harpur Hill, Mountain Rescue team 144, *145*
      Kirton in Lindsey 102, 103, 104
      Leeming 93, 96

Manston 85, 86, 88
Seighford 140, 141 *see also* Seighford, Flight Test Centre
Sutton Bridge 84, 85
Tempsford 97, 100
Wheaton Aston 140-141
Transport Command 122
Royal Aircraft Factory BE2a 20
Royal Aircraft Factory BE2c 22, 23, *23*, 24, 25
Royal Flying Corps *see also* Royal Air Force
No. 2 Squadron 20
No. 5 Wing 22-23
No. 14 Squadron 22
No. 17 Squadron 22, 23, *23*, 26
No. 29 Squadron 20, 21
Royal Naval Air Service, No. 8 Squadron 28 *see also* Royal Air Force
Ruschaert, Lieutenant 29, 32
Russell, Pilot Officer 99

Sahara Desert 22, 23-26
St George's Channel 15, 17
Sardinia 127, 128, 130, 131
Saudi Arabia 76
Savory, Major K 48
Scottish Aviation Pioneer CC1 170, 171, *171*
Seighford, Flight Test Centre 160, 161-162 *see also* Royal Air Force, stations
Seighford, 'Hollybush' pub 162
Sempill, Lord 74, *75*, 78
Seringapatam Reef 81-82
Sheffield, Lord 12, 16
Shelley, S.Sgt Guy 117, 121
Shepherd, David and Joe 104
Shiers, WH 59
Shinn, Robert 167
Shipley, Flying Officer Edwin 71
Shirt, Mrs 143-144
Short, Horace 71
Short Bros 69, 71
Calcutta 72
Kent 72, 75
Shamrock 50
Singapore III 69, *70*, 71-72, 78
Type 827: 27, 28, 29, *28-29*, *30*, 31, *31*, 32, 33
Sjoeliv 36
Smart, George 10, 11, 12, 13
Smith, Jane 76, 77
Smith, Lieutenant Keith 59
Smith, Squadron Leader Roddick Lee 102-103
Smith, Captain Ross 59
Smyth, Squadron Leader 156
Snow, Ronald E 122, 123, 125-126, *126*
Solluch, Libya 117, 118
Sopwith Atlantic 50
Sopwith Camel 47
South Pole 34, 39
Southern Cross 58, *58*, 60-61, *61*, *62*, 63, 64, *65*, 66, 67, 68
Stannage, JW 66
Star Monoplane 18, 19
Stark, Pinky 159
Steiger, HJ 73
Storhaug, Rolf 163-165, 166-167
Storm-Johnsen, Frithjof 38
Stroud, Flight Sergeant HRM 128, 129-131
Supermarine, Castle Bromwich factory 109, 110, 111
Supermarine Spitfire 109, *112*
Supermarine Spitfire Mk V 109-112, *111*
Svalbard 35, 36, 37-38, 39, *40*, 44, 45
Sweden, force-landing in 136-138

Tait, Wing Commander 134
Tanganyika, Western 27-28, 29
Tanuf, Oman 169
Taylor, PG 67
Teller, Alaska 39
Thornton, Sergeant D 100-101, *100*, *101*

Timor Sea, forced landing in 73, 81-82, *82*, *83*
Tirpitz, raids on 132-133, 134-135, 138
Tisshaw, Kingsley Peter Henry 152, 154, 155
Tjontveit, Thor 163-165, 166-167
Tombeur, General 28
Toner, Second Lieutenant Robert 117, 120-121
Toutou 28, 31
Tromsø Fjord 132, 133, 134
Trousdale, Flight Lieutenant Richard Macklow 102, 103
Turner, LAC 88
Tyler, Corporal 76

Ulm, Charles 59, 60-61, 63-64, 65-66
Umanarsuk rock 123, 125
United States Air Force bases 118-119, 120, 121, 165
United States Air Force Museum 121
United States Army Air Force 117-118

Valette, Emile 42
Valprato 56-57
Vedrines, Jules 9, 10, 11, 12, 13
Vengeur 28, 31, 32
Vickers 71
Valentia 76, 77, 78
Valetta 168, *168*, 171-172, *172*
Vellore 66
Vimy 50
Vincent 76
Wellington T10 149, 154, 155
Vire, France *100*, 101, *101*
Vivian, Charles 59

Walker, Flying Officer IHD 76, 78
Wami 28
Warner, James 60-61
weather station, Crystal Two 126
Weaver, Flight Sergeant Arthur 113, 115-116
Western Australia Airways 59, 64-65
Whalley, Sergeant J 100, *100*, *101*
Whitehouse, Jack 92
Whitley, Pilot Officer 'Bull' *87*, 88
Widdup, Pilot Officer 99
Wilkins, George Hubert 59-60
Willenhall, Stubby Lane 110-111, *111*
Williams, Pilot Officer JEM 'Bruce/Willie' 85, 86, *86*, 87, *87*, 88, 89, 90
Wimpey (George) & Co. 168, 172, *172*
Wing, monospar 73
Wireless message, first sent from the air 14
Wiseman, Sergeant 96
Wismar Bay 95
Wisting, Oscar 38
Witherick, Flying Officer Gerry A, DFM 133-134, 135, 136, 137, 139
Wolsey, HMS 95
Wolverhampton Airport 148-149, 150, 152, 155, 156
Wood, Captain Harold 'Timber' 74, 75, 78, 79, 80, 81, 82, 83
Woolner, Captain JH 48
Woravka, Second Lieutenant John 117, 121
World, first circumnavigation 66-67
Wyse, AC1 76, 78

Young, Flight Sergeant AE 'Curly' 134, 135, 137, 138
Young, Pilot Officer Mike *87*, 88, 90
Yukon, forced landing in 164-167

Zappi (*Italia* crewman) 42, 45